ARMED FORCE TRIBUNAL ACT- SUPREME COURT'S LATEST LEADING CASE LAWS

CASE NOTES- FACTS- FINDINGS OF APEX COURT JUDGES & CITATIONS

JAYPRAKASH BANSILAL SOMANI

Made with ♥ on the Notion Press Platform
www.notionpress.com

Dedicated

To

All the Past & Present Judges of the Supreme Court of India.

Salute to their wisdom.

Salute to their interpretation of Law.

Salute to their elaborative judgement writing.

Supreme Court Of India.

Contents

Contents

Preface

Dear Learned Advocates of Armed Force Tribunal, High Court and Supreme Court, Army Officers and Individuals.

I am very delighted to provide you a book on ARMED FORCE TRIBUNAL ACT- SUPREME COURT'S LATEST LEADING CASE LAWs

In this book you will get...

1. Name of the Case i. e. Cause title

2.Relevant Sections discussed in the case

3. Hon'ble Judges/Coram of the case

4.Number of PDF Pages in Original Judgement of the case

5. All available Citations of the case

6. Case Note with appeal allowed/ dismissed or disposed off

7. Facts of the case

8. Hon'ble Apex Court's findings, while dismissing/allowing or disposing the appeal

9. Ratio Decidendi if any.

My special thanks to Manupatra, because of their web portal I can compile this book in well manner. I am also thankful to Notion Press to support me to publish & market this book throughout the Country. Thanks to my Juniors, Advocate Colleagues & Insolvency Professional Colleagues to support me in this venture.

Adv. Manoj Kumar Chowdhary & Miss. Arvind Pooja Rai has helped me a lot to compile this book. I hope this book will add some value addition in the wealth of your legal knowledge. Your positive feedbacks will boost me to compile/ write further books & negative feedbacks will improve my skills. Kindly send your valuable feedbacks by email.

Thanks with Regards,

Jayprakash B. Somani

Advocate, Supreme Court of India

Email: jaysomani64@gmail.com

Web Site:www.jayprakashsomani.com

Call: 9322188701, 8459194576

Acknowledgements

Printed & Published by
Notion Press
No. 8, 3rd Cross Street,
CIT Colony, Mylapore,
Chennai, Tamil Nadu- 600004
Managed by
Jayprakash Somani Advocates & Solicitors
Law Firm for Supreme Court of India
Delhi Office
B- 851, 1st Floor, Shivaji Marg, New Ashok Nagar, Delhi 110096.
Call: 9322188701, 8459194576
Supreme Court Chamber
312, 3rd Floor, M. C. Setalvad Block, In front of 'D' Gate, Bhagwan Das Road, Supreme Court of India, New Delhi 110001
Contact: 8459194576, 9811011747
www.jayprakashsomani.com

6. E-Books/Kindle edition at National & International Level:
https://www.amazon.in/s?k=jaypraksh+somani

CHAPTER ONE

Union of India (UOI) and Ors. vs. Parashotam Dass (21.03.2023 - SC) : MANU/SC/0285/2023

Relative Section:

Air Force Act, 1950 - Section 18; Armed Forces Tribunal Act, 2007 - Section 3(o),Section 14, Section 14(1), Section 15,Section 19,Section 30, Section 30(2), Section 31, Section 32; Army Act, 1950 - Section 18; Constitution of India - Article 32, Article 136(2), Article 226, Article 227, Article 227(4), Article 323A, Article 323B,Article 368; Navy Act, 1957 - Section 15(1)

Hon'bleJudges/Coram:

Sanjay Kishan Kaul, Abhay Shreeniwas Oka and B.V. Nagarathna

Equivalent Citation: 2023/INSC/264, (2023)2MLJ653

Case Reference:

Prithi Pal Singh Bedi and Ors. v. Union of India (UOI) and Ors. MANU/SC/0233/1982;

L. Chandra Kumar v. Union of India (UOI) and Ors. MANU/SC/0261/1997;

Kesavananda Bharati Sripadagalvaru v. State of Kerala MANU/SC/0445/1973;

S.N. Mukherjee v. Union of India (UOI) MANU/SC/0346/1990;

Union of India (UOI) and Ors. v. Shri Kant Sharma and Ors. MANU/SC/0242/2015;

Rojer Mathew v. South Indian Bank Ltd. and Ors. MANU/SC/1563/2019;

Daxina Kumari v. Union of India SLP(C) No. 20721/2015;

K.C. Shibu v. Union of India SLP(C) No. 17320/2017;

Krishna Nandan Mishra v. Union of India SLP(C) No. 20499/2015;

Nand Lal Verma v. Union of India SLP(C) No. 26617/2015;

Randeep Singh Guleria v. Union of India SLP(C) No. 26568/2015;

Gopi Ram v. Union of India SLP(C) No. 26620/2015;

Avi Chander Sud v. Union of India SLP(C) No. 36386/2015;

Gurcharan Singh v. Union of India SLP(C) No. 5111/2016;

Nirmal Singh v. Union of India SLP (C) No. 28101/2016;

Davinder Singh v. Union of India SLP(C) No. 1788/2023;

Union of India v. Parashotam Dass SLP(C) No. 34797/2014;

Union of India v. Thomas Vaidyan M. Civil Appeal No. 5327/2015;

Gurbux Singh Dhindsa v. Union of India WP(C) No. 76/2016

NumberofPagesintheOriginalJudgment:12

Case Note:

Defence - Writ jurisdiction - Armed forces tribunal- Articles 226, 227, 323A and 323B of Constitution of India - Present petition filed with regard toexercise of jurisdiction under Article 226 of Constitution of India by High Court in order passed by Armed Forces Tribunal - It was submitted that exclusion of judicial review under Article 226 of Constitution ought not to be countenanced because of lack of any viable alternative appeal mechanism - Whether order passed by Armed Forces Tribunal would beamenable to challenge in writ jurisdiction under Article 226 of Constitution of India before any High Court.

Facts:

The present petition filed with regard to exercise of jurisdiction under Article 226 of Constitution of India by High Court in order passed by Armed Forces Tribunal. It was strongly contended that there could never be a bar to the exercise of jurisdiction under Article 226 of the Constitution of India by the High Court, albeit, sometimes, the High Court makes its discretion not to exercise its jurisdiction. It was further submitted that the exclusion of judicial review reviewunder Article 226 of the Constitution ought not to be countenanced because of lack of any viable alternative appeal mechanism.

Held, while disposing off the petition:

(i) This court was unable to appreciate the observations in the case of Major General Shri Kant Sharma and Anr., which sought to put an embargo on the exercise of jurisdiction under Article 226 of the Constitution, diluting a very significant provision of the Constitution which also forms the part of basic structure. The principles of basic structure have withstood the test of time and were emphasized in many judicial pronouncements as an ultimate test. This was not something that could be doubted. That being the position, the self-restraint of the High Court under Article 226 of the Constitution was distinct from putting an embargo on the High Court in exercising this jurisdiction under Article 226 of the Constitution while judicially reviewing a decision arising from an order of the Tribunal. [25]

(ii) On the legislature introducing the concept of Tribunalisation, the same was tested in L. Chandra Kumar case before a Bench of seven Judges of this Court. Thus, while upholding the principles of Tribunalisation under Article 323A or Article 323B, the Bench was unequivocally of the view that decisions of Tribunals would be subject to the jurisdiction of the High Court under Article 226of the Constitution, and would not be restricted by the forty second Constitutional Amendment which introduced the said two Articles. This should have put the matter to rest, and no Bench of less than seven Judges could have doubted the proposition. The need for the observations in the five-Judges' Bench in Rojer Mathewcase qua the Armed Forces Tribunal really arose because of the observations made in Major General Shri Kant Sharma and Anr. Thus, it was, reiterated and clarified that the power of the High Court under Article 226 of the Constitution was not inhibited, and superintendence and control under Article 227 of the Constitution were somewhat distinct from the powers of judicial review under Article 226 of the Constitution. [26]

(iii) There was no necessity to carve out certain cases from the scope of judicial review under Article 226 of the Constitution. It was enunciated in the Constitution Bench judgment in S.N. Mukherjee case that even in respect of courts-martial, the High Court could grant appropriate relief in a certain scenario as envisaged therein, i.e., if the said proceedings have resulted in denial of the fundamental rights guaranteed under Part III of the Constitution or if the said proceedings suffer from a jurisdictional error or any error of law apparent on the face of the record. [29]

CHAPTER TWO

Union of India (UOI) and Ors. vs. Vishav Priya Singh (05.07.2016 - SC) : MANU/SC/0734/2016

Relative Section:

ARMY ACT, 1950 - Section 116; Section 120

Hon'bleJudges/Coram:

T.S. Thakur, C.J.I. and U.U. Lalit

Equivalent Citation: AIR2016SC3726, 2016 6 AWC5602SC, 2016/INSC/495, 2016(6)SCALE290, (2016) 8SCC641, (2016)2SCC(LS)489, 2016 (8) SCJ 229, [2016]5SCR473, 2016(3)SCT633(SC), 2017 (3)SLR318(SC), (2016)3UPLBEC1770, (2017)2WBLR(SC)447

Case Reference:

NumberofPagesintheOriginalJudgment: 21

Case Note:

Criminal - Summary court martial - Convening of - Civil Appeal Nos. 8360 of 2010 and 8830-8835 of 2010, at instance of Union of India challenge correctness of common judgment and order of High Court of Delhi - What kind of offences could be tried by an SCM - Which CO was competent to convene, constitute and complete the SCM.

Facts:

Issue involved in present petitions was regarding SCM's convening, constitution and completion by the Commanding Officer ("CO" for short) of a Unit to which accused did not belong and circumstances in which SCM can be convened rather than a General Courts Martial ("GCM" for short), a District Courts Martial ("DCM" for short) or Summary General Courts Martial ("SGCM" for short) as envisaged in Section 108 of the Army Act 1950 (the Act). High Court held that, an SCM can legitimately be convened where there is grave and compelling cause for taking immediate action which would be defeated if reference to a District Court Martial or Summary General Court Martial is made. Holding of an SCM is the exception and not the rule

Held, while disposing off the Petitions

1. As regards SCM, Section 120 stipulates that an SCM may try any offence punishable under the Act but Sub-sections (4) and (5) limit the award of sentence. According to Sub-section (4), an SCM can pass any sentence which may be prescribed under the Act, except a sentence of death or transportation or of imprisonment of a term exceeding the limit specified in Sub-section (5). Sub-section (5) of Section 120, then prescribes the limit to the level of one year, if the officer holding the SCM is of the rank of Lieutenant Colonel and upwards and at the level of three months if the officer holding the SCM is below the rank of Lieutenant Colonel. [18]

2. Section 116 of the Act empowers CO of any Corps, Department and Detachment of regular Army to hold an SCM and specifically states that he alone shall constitute the Court. Sub-section (2) then prescribes that, proceedings shall, however, be attended through-out by two other persons specified therein. However, such persons are not to be sworn or affirmed. Unlike Sections 113, 115 and 114, where composition of the concerned Court-Martial is prescribed to consist of atleast three officers, it is the CO alone who constitutes the Court under Section 116 in respect of SCM. Further, under Rules 39 and 40 of the Rules, CO of the accused, or of the Corps to which the accused belongs is specifically disqualified for serving on a GCM or DCM and composition of a GCM ought to compose of officers of different corps or departments. However no such restriction applies to SCMs and in fact the CO himself must constitute the Court. The Act has thus given drastic power to one single individual, namely, the CO who alone is to constitute the Court. No doubt, this power comes with restrictions insofar as the power to award sentence is concerned in terms of Sub-sections (4) & (5) of Section 120. However even with such restrictions the power is quite drastic. The reason for conferment of such power is obvious that in order to maintain discipline among the soldiers and units, the CO must have certain special powers, for it is the discipline which to a great extent binds the unit and makes it a cohesive force. [19]

3. High Court of Delhi was therefore correct in observing that such power must be exercised rarely and when it is absolutely imperative that immediate action is called for. The satisfaction in that behalf must either be articulated in writing or be available on record, specially when the matter can be considered on merits by a tribunal, with the coming into force of the Armed Forces Tribunals Act, 2007.[20]

4. An SCM can try any offence punishable under the Act by virtue of Sub-section (1) of Section 120 but this general principle is subject to provisions appearing in Sub-section (2) of Section 120. Sub-section (2) of Section 120 deals with some offences in respect of which certain restrictions are applicable. The offences so stipulated are those punishable under Sections 34, 37 and 69 of the Act or those against the Officer holding the Court. Apart from Sections 34, 37 and 69 of the Act, there are various other provisions where different kinds of offences are spelt out and dealt with. For example in Chapter VI of the Act, Section 38 deals with offence of desertion, Section 39 deals with offence of absence without leave, Section 40 deals with striking or threatening a Superior Officer, Section 41 deals with disobedience to the Superior Officer, Section 42 deals with insubordination and so on. Out of multitude of such offences, only Sections 34, 37 and 69 are mentioned in Sub-section (2) in respect of which restrictions stipulated in Sub-section (2) apply. Additionally, one more category, namely "any offence against the officer holding a Court" is also specified. Such of the offences as are directed against the officer holding the Court, may include those under Sections 40, 41, 42 and so on, depending upon facts of the case. [21]

5. Sub-section (2) of Section 120 prescribes that in respect of such stipulated offences, in normal circumstances, an SCM shall not try the accused without making a reference to the officer who is otherwise empowered to convene a DCM in regular course or an SGCM while on active service. It further states that, if there is no grave reason for immediate action, such reference to the concerned officer must be made and no person should be tried without such reference in respect of any offence so stipulated i.e. those under Sections 34, 37 and 69 of the Act or those against the officer holding the Court. However no such restriction applies in cases other than Sections 34, 37, and 69 of the Act or offences against the officer holding the Court. This provision thus categorizes the offences in two compartments i.e. those which require a reference and those which do not. This distinction is also noticeable from sub Rule 2 of the Rule 22

which mandates that CO shall not dismiss a charge in respect of offences which require a reference to superior authority in terms of Section 120(2) of the Act. [22]

6. The aforesaid provision in Section 120(2) requiring a reference to the superior authority which thought is again echoed in proviso to Rule 22 (3) of the Rules, is a salutary provision and a check on exercise of drastic power conferred upon a CO and must be scrupulously observed. A case for non-adherence to this requirement must be made out on record and any deviation or non observance of statutory requirements must be viewed seriously. Offences under Sections 34, 37 and 69 of the Act are special categories or kinds of offences where a reference to the officer empowered to convene a DCM or an SGCM is considered imperative unless there are grave reasons for immediate action. Similarly, offences against the officer holding the Court, where that officer could possibly "be a judge in his own cause", are also put at the same level and similar reference under Sub-section (2) ought to be made. The exercise of power in seeking such reference and consequent consideration in respect thereof must be in keeping with the seriousness attached in respect of these offences.[23]

7. An accused committing an act constituting an offence while he was part of his regular Unit is tried by SCM by his own CO i.e., CO of the Unit itself. An accused while being on attachment to a different Unit commits an act constituting an offence and is therefore tried by SCM by the CO of such Unit to which he was sent on attachment. In such cases, offence itself would be committed while the accused was on attachment. An accused committing an act constituting an offence while being part of his regular Unit is later sent on attachment to a different Unit and is then tried by SCM by CO of such Unit i.e., Unit where he was sent on attachment after the offence was committed. [24]

8. It is not imperative that an SCM be convened, constituted and completed by CO of the Unit to which the accused belonged. It is competent and permissible for the CO of the Unit to which the accused was attached or sent on attachment for the purposes of trial, to try such accused by convening, constituting and completing SCM in a manner known to law i.e. strictly within the confines of Sections 116 and 120 of the Act and other Statutory provisions. View taken by the High Court that SCM is an exception and it is imperative that a case must be made out for immediacy of action is affirmed. The reasons to convene an SCM must be followed by well articulated reasons or the record itself must justify such resort. [33]

9. Since, High Court of Delhi had allowed Writ Petitions on short ground of competence of a CO of a Unit other than the one to which the accused belonged, without going into the merits of the matters before it, while setting aside the view in respect of that point and allowing appeals preferred by Union of India, namely Civil Appeal Nos. 8360 of 2010, 8830-8835 of 2010 and 8838 of 2010, matters remitted back to the High Court. Concerned Writ Petitions stand restored on file of the High Court for consideration on merits.[35]

CHAPTER THREE

Balkrishna Ram vs. Union of India (UOI) and Ors. (09.01.2020 - SC) : MANU/SC/0021/2020

Relative Section:

Armed Forces Tribunal Act 2007 - Section 34;

Constitution Of India - Article 214; Article 215

Hon'bleJudges/Coram:

Deepak Gupta and Aniruddha Bose, JJ.

Equivalent Citation: AIR2020SC341, 129(2020)CLT703, 2020(1)ESC91(SC), 2020/INSC/26, (2020)197PLR404, (2020)2SCC442, (2020)1SCC(LS)351, [2020]2SCR581, 2020(1)SCT576(SC), 2020(1)SLJ365(SC), 2020(4)SLR488(SC

Case Reference:

Union of India (UOI) and Ors. v. Shri Kant Sharma and Ors. MANU/SC/0242/2015; L. Chandra Kumar v. Union of India and others MANU/SC/0261/1997; W.Ex. Sigman Nand Kishore Sahoo v. Chief of Army Staff and Ors. MANU/UP/1142/2011; Union of India (UOI) v. T.R. Varma MANU/SC/0121/1957; Union of India and Ors. v. Ram Baran Special Appeal Defective No. 445 of 2005; Rojer Mathew v. South Indian Bank Ltd. and Ors. MANU/SC/1563/2019

NumberofPagesintheOriginalJudgment: 10

Case Note:

Defence - Appeal - Jurisdiction to entertain - Sections 14(1) and 34 of Armed Forces Tribunal Act, 2007 - Present appeal filed to determine jurisdiction with regard to appeal against order of Single judge of High Court deciding case related to Armed Forces personnel pending before High Court - Whether appeal against order of Single judge of High Court deciding case related to Armed Forces personnel pending before High Court was required to be transferred to Armed Forces Tribunal or should be heard by High Court.

Facts:

The present appeal had been filed to determine jurisdiction with regard to appeal against an order of a single judge of a High Court deciding a case related to an Armed Forces personnel pending before the High Court. It was contending by the Appellant that the AFT exercises all the powers of the High Court. She submits that it virtually substitutes the High Court in so far as matters governed by the Act were concerned, and as such an LPA or Special Appeal against the judgment of a single judge was also required to be transferred to the AFT.

Held, while disposing off the appeal:

(i) Section 14(1) of the Act clearly provides that the AFT will exercise powers of all courts except the Supreme Court or High Court exercising jurisdiction under Article 226 and 227 of the Constitution of India. Section 34 is very carefully worded. It states that every suit, or other proceedings pending before any court including a High Court immediately before the establishment of the Tribunal shall stand transferred on that day to the Tribunal. The Legislature had clearly not vested the AFT with the power and jurisdiction of the High Court to be exercised under Article 226 of the Constitution. The High Court could exercise its writ jurisdiction even in respect of orders passed by the AFT. True it was, that since an appeal lies to the Supreme Court against an order of the AFT, the High Court may not exercise their extraordinary writ jurisdiction because there was an efficacious alternative remedy available but that did not mean that the jurisdiction of the High Court was taken away. In a given circumstance, the High Court may and can exercise its extraordinary writ jurisdiction even against the orders of the High Court. [10]

(ii) The High Court is a Constitutional Court constituted under Article 214 of the Constitution and are courts of record within the meaning of Article 215. It was obvious that the order of the High Court could not be challenged before any other forum except the Supreme Court. The provision of intra-court appeal whether by way of Letters Patents or special enactment is a system that provides for correction of judgments within the

High Courts where a judgment rendered by a single judge may be subject to challenge before a Division Bench. This appeal to the Division Bench does not lie in all cases and must be provided for either under the Letters Patent or any other special enactment. Even where such appeal lies the appeal was heard by two or more judges of the High Court. This court could nnot envisage a situation where an appeal against the order of a sitting judge of the High Court was heard by a Tribunal comprising of one retired judge and one retired Armed Forces official. Therefore, reject the contention that an intra court appeal from the judgment of a single judge of the High Court to a Division Bench pending in the High Court was required to be transferred under Section 34 of the Act. [17]

(iii) It was not necessary to indicate in the order of discharge whether such consideration took place or not. From the records of the case, it was found that before discharge, the name of the Appellant was considered for two categories but unfortunately the Appellant could not meet the height criteria for appointment to either of the posts. Thus, this clearly shows that his case was considered as per the extant policy but he was not fit for appointment. [19]

Disposition:

Appeal Dismissed

CHAPTER FOUR

Union of India (UOI) and Ors. vs. P.S. Gill (27.11.2019 - SC) : MANU/SC/1637/2019

Relative Section:

Air Force Act, 1950 - Section 18; Armed Forces Tribunal Act, 2007 - Section 3(o), Section 14, Section 14(2), Section 15, Section 15(2), Sec31; Army Act, 1950 - Section 18, Section 52, Section 52(f), Section 63,Section 123; Constitution of India - Article 226, Article 227; Indian Evidence Act, 1872 - Section 123,Section 124; Section 175, Section 178, Section 179, Section 180, Section 193,Section 195, Section 196, Section 228; Navy Act, 1957 - Section 15(1); Army Rules, 1954 - Rule 22, Rule 23,Rule 180, Code of Criminal Procedure, 1973 (CrPC); Code of Civil Procedure, 1908 (CPC).

Hon'bleJudges/Coram:

L. Nageswara Rao and Hemant Gupta

Equivalent Citation: 2020(209)AIC59, 2020 (2) ALT (Crl.) 477 (A.P.), 2019/INSC/1290, 2019(17)SCALE111, [2019]17SCR405, 2020(1)SCT247(SC), 2020(2)SLR108(SC)

Case Reference:

State of Maharashtra v. Marwanjee P. Desai and Ors. MANU/SC/0790/2001;

Mansukhlal Dhanraj Jain and Ors. v. Eknath Vithal Ogale MANU/SC/0633/1995;

Mantri Technozone v. Forward Foundation MANU/SC/0315/2019;

S.S. Bola v. B.D. Sharma MANU/SC/0813/1997 : (1997) 2 SCC 522

NumberofPagesintheOriginalJudgment:11

Case Note:

Defence - Court martial - Jurisdiction thereto - General Court Martial was convened against Respondent on allegations pertaining to irregularities in procurement of ration, as result of which quality of supplies for troops was compromised - Respondent filed original application before Tribunal, assailing validity of order convening General Court Martial - Tribunal held that prima facie case to proceed against Respondent by General Court Martial was not made out - Appellants made attempt to obtain leave to Appeal under Section 31 of Armed Forces Tribunal Act, 2007 to approach this Court, which was not entertained - Hence, present appeal - Whether impugned order passed by Tribunal by which General Court Martial was convened against Respondent was sustainable.**Facts:**

The General Court Martial was convened allegations pertaining to irregularities in procurement of ration, as a result of which the quality of supplies for the troops was compromised. The Respondent filed original application, assailing the validity of the order convening the General Court Martial. The Tribunal held that a prima facie case to proceed against the Respondent by a General Court Martial was not made out. The Tribunal was of the opinion that even if the entirety of evidence of the prosecution was taken to be true, no offence was made out against the Respondent. The Appellants made an attempt to obtain leave to Appeal under Section 31 of the Armed Forces Tribunal Act, 2007 to approach this Court, which was not entertained.

Held, while dismissing the appeal:

(i) Any matter relating to the conditions of service falls within the definition of service matters under Section 3(o) of the Act and can be the subject matter of an application filed before the Tribunal. Conditions of service mean those conditions which regulate the holding of a post by any person right from the time of his appointment till his retirement and even after his retirement including pension etc. Therefore, conditions of service also include dismissal from service.[16]

(ii) It was clear that any proceeding which leads to an order of termination would fall within the expression relating to conditions of service. In any event, the proceedings initiated against the Respondent could not be said to be not related to his service. A final order to be passed by the General Court Martial, apart from the imposition of other penalties, might have led to the termination of the service of the Respondent.[18]

(iii) Regarding the charges sought to be framed against the Respondent, there was no error in the approach of the Tribunal. The material on record was perused by the Tribunal to come to a conclusion that no prima facie case was made out against the Respondent. There was no reason to interfere with the said findings.[21]

CHAPTER FIVE

Union of India (UOI) and Ors. vs. Virendra Kumar (07.01.2020 - SC) : MANU/SC/0005/2020

Relative Section:

Air Force Act, 1950; Armed Forces Tribunal Act, 2007 - Section 16, Section 16(2); Army Act, 1950 - Section 16,Section 64(c), Section 69; Army Rules, 1954 - Rule 22, Rule 22(1),Rule 22(3), Rule 23, Rule 177, Rule 179, Rule 180, Rule 182; Constitution of India - Article 32; Indian Penal Code, 1860 (IPC) - Section 302; Navy Act, 1957.

Hon'bleJudges/Coram:

L. Nageswara Rao and Ajay Rastogi, JJ.

Equivalent Citation: AIR2020SC422, 2020(3) ALJ 211, 2020/INSC/10, 2020LabIC847, 2020(1)RCR(Criminal)591, (2020)2SCC714, (2020)1SCC(LS)297, 2020 (4) SCJ 163, 2020(1)SLJ511(SC)

Case Reference:

Lt.-Col. Prithi Pal Singh Bedi and Ors. v. Union of India (UOI) and Ors. MANU/SC/0233/1982;

Major G.S. Sodhi v. Union of India (UOI) MANU/SC/0562/1991;

Union of India (UOI) and Ors. v. Major A. Hussain (IC-14827) MANU/SC/0874/1998; Major General Inder Jit Kumar v. Union of India (UOI) and Ors. MANU/SC/1370/1997;

Union of India (UOI) and Ors. v. Sanjay Jethi and Anr. MANU/SC/1095/2013

NumberofPagesintheOriginalJudgment: 9

Case Note:

Defence - De novo inquiry - Denial of - Rule 180 of Army Rules, 1954 and Sections 16(2),64(c) and 69 of Army Act, 1950 - Disciplinary action initiated against Respondent for causing death of soldier and for attempting to commit suicide - Respondent was tentatively charged with murder under Section 302 of Code read with Section 69 of Act and Section 64(c) of Act for attempting to commit suicide - General Court Martial convicted Respondent under Section 302 of Code and for attempting to commit suicide - Respondent was sentenced to suffer imprisonment for life and to be dismissed from service - Statutory complaint filed by Respondent was rejected - Validity of order of General Court was assailed before Tribunal - Tribunal held that as Respondent was denied permission to be present when statements of witnesses were being recorded before Court of Inquiry, Tribunal set aside order of Court Martial and remitted matter for de novo - Hence, present appeal - Whether Tribunal erred in remanding matter back for a de novo inquiry on ground of infraction of Rule 180 of Rules.

Facts:

The disciplinary action to be initiated against the Respondent for causing the death of soldier and for attempting to commit suicide. The Respondent was tentatively charged with the murder under Section 302 Indian Penal Code read with Section 69 of the Army Act, 1950 and under Section 64(c) of the Act for attempting to commit suicide. The General Court Martial commenced and the trial was concluded. The General Court Martial convicted the Respondent under Section 302 Indian Penal Code for the murder and for attempting to commit suicide. The Respondent was sentenced to suffer imprisonment for life and to be dismissed from service. The statutory complaint filed by the Respondent was rejected by the Chief of the Army Staff. The validity of the order of the General Court Martial and the order of the Chief of the Army Staff rejecting the statutory complaint were assailed before the Tribunal. As there was no doubt that the Respondent was denied permission to be present when statements of witnesses were being recorded before the Court of Inquiry, the Tribunal concluded that the entire trial against the Respondent is vitiated. The Tribunal set aside the order of the Court Martial and remitted the matter for de novo trial from the stage of Court of Inquiry in exercise of its power under Section 16 of the Armed Forces Tribunal Act, 2007.

Held, while allowing the appeal:

(i) Though there was non-compliance of Rule 180 of the Army Rules in this case as the Respondent was not present during the recording of the statements of witnesses, it was clear from the record that the Respondent did not raise this ground either at the stage of framing of the charge, recording summary of evidence or during the Court Martial proceedings. After a final order was passed by the Court Martial on the basis of a full-fledged trial, it was not open to the Respondent to raise the ground of non-compliance of Rule 180 during the Court of Inquiry proceedings. Therefore, the Tribunal ought not to have remanded the matter back for a de novo inquiry from the stage of Court of Inquiry on the ground of infraction of Rule 180 of the Army Rules. [13]

(ii) The power conferred on the Tribunal to direct re-trial by the Court Martial was only on the grounds mentioned in Section 16(2). The Tribunal was competent to direct re-trial only in case of evidence made available to the Tribunal was not produced before the Court Martial and if it appears to the Tribunal that the interests of justice requires a re-trial. The re-trial that was ordered by the Tribunal in this case was on the basis that the procedure prescribed in Rule 180 of the Army Rules had not been followed. The Tribunal did not have jurisdiction to direct re-trial on any other ground except that mentioned in Section 16(2). Non-compliance of Rule 180 could not be a ground for ordering a re-trial. In addition, the Tribunal had competence only to order re-trial by the Court Martial. There was no power conferred on the Tribunal to direct the matter to be remanded to a stage prior to the Court Martial proceedings. Therefore, the order passed by the Tribunal directing a de novo inquiry from the stage of Court of Inquiry requires to be set aside. [15]

Disposition:

Appeal Allowed

CHAPTER SIX

Union of India (UOI) and Ors. vs. Annie Nagaraja and Ors. (17.03.2020 - SC) : MANU/SC/0307/2020

Relative Section:

Armed Forces Tribunal Act 2007 - Section 19,Section 30, Section 30(1), Section 30(2),Section 31, Section 31(1), Section 31(2); Army Act, 1950 - Section 21, Army Rules, 1954; Constitution of India - Article 19 (1),Article 14, Article 21, Article 33,Article 142,Article 203,Article 226; Naval Ceremonial, Conditions of Service and Miscellaneous Regulations 1963 - Regulation 122,122(1), 122(14),122(2),122(9),124, 124(14), 124(2), 126, 126(14), 126(2), 202, 203, 203(1); Navy Act, 1957 - Section 9,Section 9(2), Section 184, Section 185.

Hon'ble Judges/Coram:

Dr. D.Y. Chandrachud and Ajay Rastogi, JJ.

Equivalent Citation: 2020/INSC/300, (2020)3MLJ388, (2020)13SCC1, (2021)1SCC(LS)169, [2020]10SCR433, 2020(2)SCT444(SC), 2020(6)SLR817(SC)

Case Reference:

Gangai Vinayagar Temple v. Meenakshi Ammal MANU/SC/0926/2014; Union of India (UOI) and Ors. v. Brigadier P.S. Gill MANU/SC/0234/2012; Lt.-Col. Prithi Pal Singh Bedi and Ors. v. Union of India (UOI) and Ors. MANU/SC/0233/1982; R. Viswan and Ors. v. Union of India (UOI) and Ors. MANU/SC/0338/1983; Union of India (UOI) and Ors. v. L.D. Balam Singh MANU/SC/0360/2002; Mohd. Yunus Khan v. State of U.P. and Ors.

MANU/SC/0767/2010; Babita Puniya v. Union of India Writ Petition (C) No. 1597 of 2013;Priya Khurana v. Union of India; The Secretary, Ministry of Defence v. Babita Puniya MANU/SC/0194/2020 : 2020 (3) SCALE 712

NumberofPagesintheOriginalJudgment: 38

Case Note:

Defence - Permanent Commission - Grant of - Regulations 122(2), 124(2) and 126(2) and 203 of Naval Ceremonial, Conditions of Service and Miscellaneous Regulations 1963 and Section 9(2) of Navy Act 1957 - Ministry of Defence issued policy letter granting PCs to SSC officers in all three branches of Armed Forces - However, offer was restricted to certain categories and was to operate prospectively for benefit of future batches inducted on SSCs - Petitioners, were women officers who joined the Indian Navy as Short Service Commissioned Officers - Writ petition was filed before High Court - High Court held that claim of absorption in areas of operation not open for recruitment of women officers could not be sustained being policy decision - It was further held that Short Service Commissioned Officers of Navy who had opted for PC and were not granted PC but instead were granted extension of SSC - In similar matters, Armed Forces Tribunal (AFT) disagreed with direction of High Court for grant of PCs and directed authorities to consider cases of SSC officers for grant of PCs - Hence, present appeal - Whether women in Indian Navy entitled to Permanente Commission.

Facts:

The Union of India in the Ministry of Defence issued a policy letter granting PCs to SSC officers in all the three branches of the Armed Forces. However, the offer was restricted to certain categories and was to operate prospectively for the benefit of future batches inducted on SSCs. The High Court held that the claim of absorption in areas of operation not open for recruitment of women officers could not be sustained being a policy decision. It was further held that the Short Service Commissioned Officers of the Navy who had opted for PC and were not granted PC but instead were granted extension of SSC and were not retired at the time of filing of these Writ Petitions and had attained the age of retirement during the pendency of the present petitions, they shall be offered PC. In similar matters, the Armed Forces Tribunal (AFT) disagreed with the direction of the High Court for the grant of PCs and directed the authorities to consider the cases of the SSC officers for the grant of PCs. The AFT was of the view that as it did not possess the requisite expertise and necessary materials for determining whether PCs should be granted, such a decision must be left to the relevant authorities. However, the AFT directed that until such consideration was made and a decision was taken, the applicants before it would be allowed to continue as SSC officers on existing terms and conditions as applicable to them.

Held, while disposing off the appeal:

(i) The course of the evolution of policy clearly indicates a legitimate expectation on part of the SSC officers (both men and women) of being governed by the provisions of Regulation 203 being considered for the grant of PCs. The Navy Regulations, when they were originally drafted in 1963, did not contemplate the induction of women. For this reason, Regulations 122(2), 124(2) and 126(2) spoke of only unmarried males being eligible for induction on SSCs. The Regulations being subservient to statute, incorporated restrictions which comported with the provisions of Section 9(2). However, what Section 9(2) envisages is that the restrictions on the enrolment or appointment of women in branches or departments of the Indian Navy would be lifted upon the issuance of a notification by the Union Government sanctioning the entry of women officers, subject to the conditions which may be specified. Both in the notifications, the Union Government lifted the statutory bar in exercise of its enabling power under Section 9(2) by allowing for the entry for women as officers in the Indian Navy in stipulated branches. Once the statutory bar stood lifted, the appointment of SSC officers, both men and women on PCs would be governed uniformly by the provisions of Regulation 203. This was made abundantly clear by the policy letter which was issued in compliance with the legal regime. The grant of PCs to SSC men and women officers aligned with the provisions of Regulation 203 which plainly is a matter of law. Thus, the contention urged that the communication was merely anticipatory in nature and that the entitlement to be considered for the grant of PCs would have to await a further policy, could not be accepted. The communication of the MoD had the sanction of the President and consequently cannot be disregarded as suggested in the arguments urged by the Union of India in these proceedings. [65]

(ii) The policy decision of the MoD governed the grant of PCs to SSC women officers in the Army, Navy and Air Force. The communication, by stipulating that it would apply to SSC women officers to be inducted, purported to exclude women SSC officers in service from being considered for the grant of PCs. It also sought to restrict the cadres/branches in which

PCs could be granted to women SSC officers. The AFT had noted after it had summoned the files, that the earlier policy decision was not placed before the decision making authorities. The AFT concluded that while a policy framed by the government was amenable to change or alteration, decision making by the government is subject to the norms of reasonableness and a non-arbitrary exercise of power. Evidently, in the view of the AFT, the decision was not a conscious departure from the earlier policy. It could not have been a conscious departure for the simple reason that the earlier policy was not evaluated nor was there any basis formulated to justify a departure from it. Quite apart from this however, there was a more fundamental reason why a finding in regard to the invalidity of the policy letter in relation to the Navy rests on a sure foundation. The 1963 Regulations contain specific provisions in regard to the grant of SSCs and for the grant of PCs. Regulations 122, 124 and 126 govern the grant of SSCs, while Regulation 203 governs the grant of PCs. Regulation 203, in its own terms, is not restricted in its application to only male officers. Once the appointment of women officers in the Indian Navy was permitted in terms of the statutory notifications, the statutory bar under Section 9(2) stood lifted and women officers inducted on SSCs would be entitled to be governed by Regulation 203. Hence, the policy letter to the extent it seeks to restrict the grants of PCs to specified cadres/branches as well as only to women officers to be inducted was contrary to the notifications and shall not be enforced. The policy letter was not in supersession of the statutory notifications. At the highest it may be construed as an administrative decision to implement the statutory notifications. Hence, it could not be construed to be prospective in character as any other view to the contrary would be in violation of Section 9(2) of the Act. The conclusion which was arrived at by the High Court and by AFT was unimpeachable in its logical consistency and is in keeping with the legal regime envisaged by the 1957 Act, the 1963 Regulations and the notifications issued. [67]

(iii) Once the policy decision of the Union Government was communicated, the authorities were bound to consider the claims of the SSC officers for the grant of PC in terms of Regulation 203. The naval authorities and the Union Government failed to do so, depriving them of the entitlement to be considered for the grant of PC. By the failure of the authorities to consider the SSC officers for PCs in terms of the policy communication, SSC officers lost out on the opportunity to be granted PCs and all the responsibilities and benefits attached to the grant of PC, including promotions and pensionable service. The situation which had come to pass is due to the failure of the authorities to implement statutory notifications issued under Section 9(2) the policy statement by which they were bound and as the decisions of the High Court and the AFT. These SSC officers could not be left in the lurch and the injustice meted to them by lost years of service and the deprivation of retiral entitlements must be rectified. The injustice is a direct consequence of the authorities having breached their duties under law. To deny substantive relief to the SSC officers would result in a situation where a breach of duty on the part of the authorities to comply with binding legal norms would go unattended. This would result in a serious miscarriage of justice to the SSC officers who had served the nation and was unsustainable in law. [91]

(iv) The right of women SSC officers to be considered for the grant of PCs in the Logistics and Education cadres arose by virtue of the policy letter. The non-consideration of the case of these five officers for the grant of PCs arose out of the actions of the Union Government in issuing a restricted policy which had caused serious prejudice to these women officers. These officers were among the first inductee batches of women SSC officers in the Navy and committed themselves to serving in the cause of the nation. The second to sixth Respondents who had been released had been out of service for twelve years and more. Consistent with the exigencies of service, it would not be appropriate to direct their reinstatement. However, following the logic of the directions of this Court in Babita Puniya, a one-time measure should be issued in exercise of the powers under Article 142 of the Constitution. These officers who were released after completing their engagement should be deemed to have completed substantive pensionable service and to have qualified for the grant of pension on the basis that they had fulfilled the minimum qualifying service in a substantive capacity. In addition to the grant of pensionary benefits, as a one-time measure, Respondents two to six should be directed to be paid a lump sum amount as compensatory measure for lost years of service and the serious injustice which has been meted out to them. The decision to award compensation was not a reflection of any malice on the part of the Naval authorities but a measure of compensation for the women officers who had been deprived of a valuable opportunity to render service and shoulder responsibilities. [95]

(v) Therefore, it was direct that:

(a) The statutory bar on the engagement or enrolment of women in the Indian Navy had been lifted to the extent envisaged in the notifications issued by the Union Government under Section 9(2) of the 1957 Act.

(ii) By and as a result of the policy decision of the Union Government in the Ministry of Defence, the terms and conditions of service of SSC officers, including women in regard to the grant of PCs were governed by Regulation 203, Chapter IX, Part III of the 1963 Regulations.

(iii) The stipulation in the policy letter making it prospective and restricting its application to specified cadres/branches of the Indian Navy shall not be enforced.

(iv) The provisions of the implementation guidelines, to the extent that they were made prospective and restricted to specified cadres were quashed and set aside.

(v) All SSC officers in the Education, Law and Logistics cadres who were presently in service shall be considered for the grant of PCs. The right to be considered for the grant of PCs arises from the policy letter read with Regulation 203 of Chapter IX Part III of the 1963 Regulations. SSC women officers in the batch of cases before the High Court and the AFT, who were presently in service shall be considered for the grant of PCs on the basis of the vacancy position as on the date of judgments of the High Court and the AFT or as it presently stands, whichever is higher.

(vi) The period of service after which women SSC officers shall be entitled to submit applications for the grant of PCs shall be the same as their male counterparts.

(vii) The applications of the serving officers for the grant of PCs shall be considered on the basis of the norms contained in Regulation 203 namely availability of vacancies in the stabilised cadre at the material time, determination of suitability and recommendation of the Chief of the Naval Staff. Their empanelment shall be based on inter se merit evaluated on the ACRs of the officers under consideration, subject to the availability of vacancies.

(viii) SSC officers who were found suitable for the grant of PC shall be entitled to all consequential benefits including arrears of pay, promotions and retiral benefits as and when due. [96]

CHAPTER SEVEN

The Secretary, Ministry of Defence vs. Babita Puniya and Ors. (17.02.2020 - SC) : MANU/SC/0194/2020

Relative Section:

Army Act, 1950 - Section 10,Section-12, Section 21,Section 69,Section 125; Constitution of India - Article 14, Article 15(1),Article 16(1),Article 19, Article 19(1), Article 21, Article 33, Article 136; Indian Penal Code, 1860 (IPC) - Section 302; Army Rules, 1954.

Hon'bleJudges/Coram:

Dr. D.Y. Chandrachud and Ajay Rastogi,

EquivalentCitation:AIR2020SC1000,2020/INSC/198,2020(4)MhLj356,(2020)2MLJ343,2020(4)MPLJ 273, (2020)7SCC469, (2020)2SCC(LS)801, 2020 (6) SCJ 90, [2020]3SCR833, 2020(2)SCT207(SC), 2020(3) SLJ75(SC), 2020(5)SLR59(SC)

Case Reference:

Ram Sarup v. The Union of India (UOI) and Anr. MANU/SC/0047/1963;

Lt.-Col. Prithi Pal Singh Bedi and Ors. v. Union of India (UOI) and Ors. MANU/SC/0233/1982;

R. Viswan and Ors. v. Union of India (UOI) and Ors. MANU/SC/0338/1983;

Union of India v. P K Chaudhary Civil Appeal No 3208 of 2015

NumberofPagesintheOriginalJudgment:31

Case Note:

Service - Grant of PC - Section 12 of Army Act, 1950 - Present appeal has been filed for challenging HC's order directing that the Short Service Commissioned women officers are entitled to PC at par with male Short Service Commissioned officers with all consequential benefits - During the pendency of this appeal, MoD issued a communication for the grant of PCs to SSC women officers in 10 arms or services of the Army including JAG and AEC - UOI also tendered a proposal which envisages certain directions related to pension of women - Whether women entitled to get Permanent Commission in the Indian Army? - Whether the communication dated 25th February 2019 issued by MoD should be implemented?

Facts:

On 30th January 1992, Union of India (UOI) has issued a notification making women eligible for appointment as officers in the specific branches/cadres of the Army for five years. The initial period of five years was later on extended by a notification dated 12th December 1996 issued by Ministry of Defence (MoD). In February 2003, Babita Puniya, an advocate instituted a Writ Petition in the nature of a Public Interest Litigation before the Delhi High Court for the grant of PC to women Short Service Commission (SSC) officers in the Army.

On 28th October 2005, a notification was issued by the MoD by which the UOI extended the validity of the scheme of appointment of women as officers in the Indian Army and the tenure of women officers inducted under the Women Special Entry Scheme (Officers) (WSES) was extended by five years. During the course of the proceedings, two circulars were issued on 20th July 2006, conveying the sanction of the President of India regarding the grant of SSCs both on the technical and non-technical side to women officers for 14 years. Various petitions filed for seeking the grant of PCs for women officers. By a judgment dated 12th March 2010, the High Court directed that the Short Service Commissioned women officers are entitled to PC at par with male Short Service Commissioned officers with all consequential benefits. Assailing the judgment, the Union of India (UOI) has approached the present court.

Held:

(i) On a textual interpretation of Section 12 of the Act as it stands, it is evident that the policy decision dated 25 February 2019 of the Union Government has allowed for the grant of PCs to commissioned women officers in all the ten streams which have been notified.

(ii) The policy decision of the Union Government is a recognition of the right of women officers to equality of opportunity. One facet of that right is the principle of non-discrimination on the ground of sex which is embodied in Article 15(1) of the Constitution. The second facet of the right is equality of opportunity for all citizens in matters of public employment under Article 16(1) of Constitution. The policy statement of the Union Government must therefore be construed as a decision which enforces the fundamental right of women to seek access to public appointment and to equality of opportunity in matters of engagement relating to the Army.

(iii) The salient decision of the Union Government to extend PCs to women SSC officers in all ten streams in which they are commissioned is a step forward in recognising and realising the right of women to equality of opportunity in the Army. This marks a step towards realising the fundamental constitutional commitment to the equality and dignity of women.

(iv) There is fundamental fallacy in the distinction which has been sought to be drawn between women officers with less than fourteen years of service with those with service between fourteen and twenty years and above twenty years. The judgment of the Delhi High Court was rendered on 12 March 2010. The Union Government was duty bound to enforce the judgment of the Delhi High Court, the judgment not having been stayed during the pendency of these appeals. The failure of the government to implement the judgment of the Delhi High Court has caused irreparable prejudice to the women officers as they have lost the benefit of promotions and the assumption of higher responsibilities as members of the Armed Force. Thus, SSC women officers, both within the period of fourteen years' service and beyond, should equally be entitled to consideration for the grant of PCs.

(v) The policy decision which has been taken by the Union Government on 25 February 2019 indicates that it is to apply prospectively. It is necessary here to clarify that the prospective application of the decision does not mean that it would apply to women officers who have been appointed as SSCs officers after the date of the decision. Thus, the policy decision will apply to all women SSC officers who are currently in service irrespective of the length of service which has been rendered by them.

(vi) The next aspect of the policy decision relates to the restriction which has been imposed on women officers being granted PCs for staff appointments. Such a restriction was not imposed when the JAG and AEC branches were opened up for the grants of PCs for women SSC officers in the past. The consequence of this, is an implicit acceptance by the Army that women can, in certain situations, receive criteria or command appointments. An absolute bar on women seeking criteria or command appointments would not comport with the guarantee of equality under Article 14 of Constitution. Implicit in the guarantee of equality is that where the action of the State does differentiate between two classes of persons, it does not differentiate them in an unreasonable or irrational manner. In this sense, even at its bare minimum, the right to equality is a right to rationality. Where the State, and in this case the Army as an instrumentality of the State, differentiates between women and men, the burden falls squarely on the Army to justify such differentiation with reason. An absolute prohibition of women SSC officers to obtain anything but staff appointments evidently does not fulfill the purpose of granting PCs as a means of career advancement in the Army. Whether a particular candidate should or should not be granted a criteria or command assignment is a matter for the competent authority to consider having regard to all the exigencies of service, performance and organisational requirements. In the present case the Army has provided no justification in discharging its burden as to why women across the board should not be considered for any criteria or command appointments. Command assignments are not automatic for men SSC officers who are granted PC and would not be automatic for women either. The absolute exclusion of women from all others except staff assignments in indefensible. If the army has cogent reasons for excluding women from a particular criteria or command appointment, it may provide them to the relevant authorities and if necessary, to future courts. However, such a justification must take place on a case-to-case basis, in light of the requirements and exigencies of a particular appointment. The blanket non-consideration of women for criteria or command appointments absent an individuated justification by the Army cannot be sustained in law. Thus, the expression "in various staff appointments only" in paragraph 5 and that "on staff appointments only" in paragraph 6 of the communication dated 25 February 2019 shall not be enforced.

(vii) Appeals disposed of with following directions: (i) The policy decision which has been taken by the Union Government allowing for the grant of PCs to SSC women officers in all the ten streams where women have been granted SSC in the Indian Army is accepted subject to some conditions. (ii) SSC women officers who are granted PC in pursuance of the above directions will be entitled to all consequential benefits including promotion and financial benefits. However, these benefits would be made available to those officers in service or those who had moved the Delhi High Court by filing the Writ Petitions and those who had retired during the course of the pendency of the proceedings. Necessary steps for compliance with this judgment directed to be taken within three months from the date of this judgment.

Disposition:

Disposed of

CHAPTER EIGHT

Mohammed Ansari vs. Union of India (UOI) and Ors. (02.02.2017 - SC) : MANU/SC/0106/2017

Relative Section:

Administrative Tribunals Act, 1985 - Section 2,Section 3; Armed Forces Tribunal Act 2007 - Section 2,Section 2(1), Section 3, Section 14; Army Act, 1950 - Section 3, Army Act, 1950 - Section 4, Army Act, 1950 - Section 4(1), Army Act, 1950 - Section 4(4), Army Act, 1950 - Section 5, Army Act, 1950 - Section 10, Army Act, 1950 - Section 11, Army Act, 1950 - Section 13, Army Act, 1950 - Section 14, Army Act, 1950 - Section 15, Army Act, 1950 - Section 16, Army Act, 1950 - Section 17, Army Act, 1950 - Section 18, Army Act, 1950 - Section 20, Army Act, 1950 - Section 21, Army Act, 1950 - Section 22, Army Act, 1950 - Section 23, Army Act, 1950 - Section 24, Army Act, 1950 - Section 29, Army Act, 1950 - Section 43, Army Act, 1950 - Section 44, Army Act, 1950 - Section 71, Army Act, 1950 - Section 74, Army Act, 1950 - Section 75, Army Act, 1950 - Section 76, Army Act, 1950 - Section 77, Army Act, 1950 - Section 78, Army Act, 1950 - Section 80, Army Act, 1950 - Section 84; Navy Act, 1957 - Section 15(1); Air Force Act, 1950 - Section 18; Central Civil Services (Control, Classification and Appeal) Rules, 1965 - Rule 19; Army Rules, 1954; Constitution of India - Article 14, Article 33,Article 226, Article 227.

Hon'bleJudges/Coram:

Dipak Misra and U.U. Lalit,

Equivalent Citation: 245(2017)DLT191, 2017(3)ESC503(SC), [2017(155)FLR767], (2017)2MLJ688, 2017(2)SCALE154, (2017)3SCC740, (2017)1SCC(LS)761, [2017]1SCR422, 2017(2)SCT61(SC), 2017(4)SLR740(SC)

Case Reference:

Ramkali Mishra and Ors. v. Union of India;

R. Viswan and Ors. v. Union of India & Ors. MANU/SC/0338/1983 :

(1983) 3 SCC 401 : AIR 1983 SC 558; Union of India v. Smt. Vidyawati S.L.P. (C) No. 8096 of 1995;

Union of India and Ors. v. Sunil Kumar Sarkar MANU/SC/0148/2001 : (2001) 3 SCC 414;

L. Chandra Kumar v. Union of India MANU/SC/0261/1997 : (1997) 3 SCC 261;

Union of India v. G.S. Grewal MANU/SC/0517/2014 : (2014) 7 SCC 303;

Sub. Inspector Rooplal v. Lt. Governer MANU/SC/0776/1999 : (2000) 1 SCC 644;

Hiralal Moolchand Doshi v. Barot Raman Lal Ranchhoddas MANU/SC/0225/1993 : (1993) 2 SCC 458;

Major General S.B. Akali Case TA No. 125 of 2010

NumberofPagesintheOriginalJudgment:15

Case Note:

Service - Jurisdiction of Tribunal - Original application - Entertaining thereof - Article 226 of Constitution of India and Armed Forces Tribunal Act, 2007 - Appellant was not granted non-functional financial upgradation - Appellant preferred application before Tribunal - Respondent filed preliminary objection regarding jurisdiction of Tribunal - The Tribunal decided issue in favour of Appellant - Tribunal opined that it has jurisdiction to entertain original application - Respondents preferred petition seeking quashment of order passed by Tribunal - High Court held that Tribunal has/had no jurisdiction in present matter - Hence, present appeal - Whether after coming into force of Act, 2007 it will be Armed Forces Tribunal which shall deal with controversy or High Court would still have original jurisdiction under Article 226 of Constitution

Facts:

The Appellant was appointed as an Assistant Executive Engineer in Border Roads Engineering Services by the competent authority of the Government of India. In due course, he was promoted to the post of

Executive Engineer (E & M) and thereafter promoted to the grade of Superintending Engineer (E & M) in General Reserve Engineering Force (GREF) of Border Roads Organization. The Appellant after completion of more than requisite years of service was not granted non-functional financial upgradation for officers of Organised Group A and that compelled him to make representation to the concerned authorities but the same were turned down on the ground that he had not fulfilled the stipulated command posting of two years. Being aggrieved by the said communication, the Appellant preferred application before the Tribunal. The Respondent filed a preliminary objection regarding jurisdiction of the Tribunal. The Tribunal decided the issue in favour of the Appellant. The Tribunal referred to its own decision in Ramkali Mishra and Ors. v. Union of India. The Tribunal opined that it has jurisdiction to entertain the original application. The Respondents preferred the petition seeking quashment of the order passed by the Tribunal. The High Court that as far as Central Administrative Tribunal is concerned, a member of the GREF is not covered, in the light of the decision in R. Viswan and Ors. v. Union of India and Ors. read with the decision in Union of India v. Smt. Vidyawati, by the provisions of the Administrative Tribunals Act, 1985, and, hence, a member of the GREF would be disentitled from invoking the jurisdiction of the Central Administrative Tribunal. It was held that the Central Administrative Tribunal has/had no jurisdiction in the present matter.

Held, while dismissing the appeal:

(i) The proceedings under the Army Act, 1950 as well as the Central Civil Services (Control, Classification and Appeal) Rules, 1965 are maintainable and do not amount to double jeopardy. The principle that is deducible is that the person aggrieved under the 1950 Act at that juncture can approach High Court and similarly, the same person aggrieved by the imposition of punishment under the disciplinary proceeding can challenge the same Under Article 226 of the Constitution before the High Court. Thus, it is graphically clear that this Court did not think that the aggrieved party can agitate the grievance before the Central Administrative Tribunal under the 1985 Act. [13]

(ii) The Circular issued by the Government of India in exercise of its power Under Section 4(1) of the 1950 Act carves out certain exceptions. These exceptions include the GREF from purview of the 1950 Act in certain cases pertaining to service matters, in particular. The exceptions clearly show that the 1950 Act has not been applied in entirety to the members of

GREF. [15]

(iii) The language of the provisions of the 1985 Act is absolutely plain and the Act does not apply to any member of the armed forces and, therefore, the High Court is justified in holding that Central Administrative Tribunal does not have the jurisdiction to deal with the controversy. [18]

(iv) The statement of objects and reasons of the Act, 2007 as is manifest, mandates adjudication of complaints and disputes regarding service matters of the members of the Armed Forces. The members of the GREF belong to the Armed Forces. The constitution of GREF has to be appreciated. It is a departmental construction agency responsible to build and maintain roads in the North and North Eastern border areas of the country. It is different from other construction agencies like CPWD, PWD, etc, inasmuch as, it is a Force raised and maintained by the Central Government to support the Army in latter's operational role at the border areas. The GREF functions under the Border Road Development Board, and its Units are modeled on the lines of Army Units/Sub Units like Task Force, Road Construction Companies, Road Maintenance Platoons etc. [24]

(v) R. Viswan is an authority to the extent that the members of GREF though may be termed as civilian officers, yet by the very nature of the organisation, are treated to be an integral part of the Armed Forces within the meaning of Article 33 of the Constitution of India and would be subjected to penal action under the provisions of the 1950 Act and Army Rules, 1954 and disciplinary action under CCS (CCA) Rules, 1965. [25]

(vi) The 1950 Act and the Army Rules, 1954 have been applied to civilian personnel of the GREF only for the purpose of discipline. The reasons are obvious. The GREF is a force raised and maintained under the authority of the Central Government, its units are set up on the lines of the Indian Army, it works with and under close coordination with regular army in border areas, facilitates the Indian Army to carry out its operational role, etc. Hence, it has been felt appropriate that the 1950 Act should be made applicable to a force raised and maintained by the Central Government as considered necessary in the interest of discipline. The issue can be perceived from a different perspective. The GREF personnel are subjected by legislative scheme to dual disciplinary control, and such an arrangement is permissible as has been held in R. Viswan. When the offence is such that the provisions of the 1950 Act, as extended to GREF, apply for the purpose of discipline, it will be open to the competent disciplinary authority under the 1950 Act, to proceed against the delinquent under its provisions, and if found guilty, award appropriate punishment. If an offence is committed in relation to an enemy, offences on active service, mutiny, desertion, disobedience, etc., considering the nature and gravity of the offence, it may warrant severe action against the delinquent by way of trial by a court martial. In other disciplinary cases, the competent authority may decide to proceed under CCS(CCA) Rules, 1965 in which the maximum permissible punishment is only 'dismissal from service'. [30]

(vii) The 2007 Act has been made applicable to persons subject to the 1950 Act, the Navy Act, 1957 and the Air Force Act, 1950, the retired personnel subject to these Acts including their dependants, heirs and successors insofar as it relates to their service matters. The Tribunal constituted in terms of Sections 4 and 5 thereof, is vested with twin jurisdiction viz., jurisdiction, powers and authority in service matters as provided in Section 14 and the jurisdiction in matter of appeal against courts martial Under Section 15 of the Act. [31]

(viii) The AFT shall have jurisdiction (i) to hear appeals arising out of courts martial verdicts qua GREF personnel. To this extent alone the AFT shall have jurisdiction. At the same time if the punishment is imposed on GREF personnel by way of departmental proceedings held under the CCS(CCA) Rules, 1965 the same cannot be agitated before the AFT and (ii) AFT shall have no jurisdiction to hear and decide grievances of GREF personnel relating to their terms and conditions of service or alternatively put 'service matters'. During the pendency of the matter before the High Court, the Central Administrative Tribunal had passed the final order in favour of the Appellant. The Tribunal does not have the jurisdiction to deal with an issue of upgradation or the nature of lis raised by the Appellant before it. In the absence of lack of inherent jurisdiction to deal with the issue, the said judgment was a nullity. It had no existence in law. It is well settled in law that the judgment passed is a nullity if it is passed by a court having no inherent jurisdiction. [33] and[34]

Prior History / High Court Status:

From the Judgment and Order dated 02.08.2013 of the High Court of Guwahati in Writ Petition (C) No. 4074 of 2012 (MANU/GH/0255/2013)

Disposition:

Appeal Dismissed

CHAPTER NINE

Navtej Singh vs. Union of India (UOI) and Ors. (05.12.2018 - SC) : MANU/SC/1424/2018

Relative Section:

Armed Forces Tribunal Act 2007 - Section 30; Armed Forces Tribunal Act 2007 - Section 31(2); Citizenship Act, 1955; Air Force Act, 1950.

Hon'bleJudges/Coram:

U.U. Lalit and Dr. D.Y. Chandrachud, JJ.

Equivalent Citation: 2018(4)ESC760(SC), 2018/INSC/1157, (2019)1MLJ731, 2018(15) SCALE603 , (2019)3SCC345, (2019)1SCC(LS)443, [2018]14SCR665, 2019(1)SCT204(SC), 2019(2) SLR813(SC)

Case Reference: nil

NumberofPagesintheOriginalJudgment: 9

Case Note:

Civil - Post-retirement benefits - Present appeals under Section 30 read with Section 31(2) of Armed Forces Tribunal Act, 2007 (" Act",) were directed against (i) judgment dated 24th February, 2015 in O.A. No. 420/ 2013 and (ii) judgment and order dated 3rd July, 2015 in Review Application No. 19/2015 in O.A. No. 420/2013; passed by Tribunal. Whether names of Appellant's family members (wife and daughter) was liable to be recorded in service record and allow all benefits due to them -Whether marriage of Petitioner with Meenu Sangha could be recognized for purposes of grant of post-retirement benefits, medical facilities and family pension etc.

Facts:

Appellant after completing training from Air Force Academy, Hyderabad, was granted commission in rank of Pilot Officer in branch of Flying Navigation of Indian Air Force with effect from 16th December, 1995. Thereafter, he received promotions in due course of time and was finally promoted to rank of Squadron Leader. Sometime in year 2001, Appellant was diagnosed of Dysmia and Alcohol Dependence Syndrome and Primary Hypothyroidism and since n was put in low medical category. A Medical Board was constituted to consider his medical condition and Medical Board found him to be unfit for all flying duties. Appellant was given option of being transferred to Administrative Branch but expressed his unwillingness. In circumstances, Invaliding Medical Board was constituted to consider case which declared that, Appellant be invalidated out of service on medical grounds. Aforesaid recommendation of Invaliding Medical Board was approved and Appellant was invalidated out of service with effect from 18th November, 2009 in rank of Squadron Leader. While in service, on 27th October, 2008 Appellant had applied to Director, Directorate of IMINT, Air Headquarters (VB), New Delhi, seeking permission to marry. Tribunal did not accept case that, medical condition of Appellant was attributable to or was aggravated by conditions of service. It however held that, Appellant had 30% disability which was to be rounded off to 50% and consequently was entitled to disability pension @ 50% with interest @ 12% per annum. It however rejected case that, Appellant was entitled to promotion as claimed. It was also held that since marriage was contracted by Appellant without any permission, he was not entitled to take benefit of his marriage with foreign national. Tribunal thus partly allowed O.A. No. 420/2013. Appellant thereafter filed Review Application No. 19/2015 seeking review on grounds that Appellant had applied for ex-post facto sanction of marriage on 15.01.2009 which was duly recommended by Section Commander and Air Officer Commanding. It was further stated that, in terms of AFO 14/2000, Respondents had to process application within 120 days and as there was complete failure on their part, in terms of said AFO, there would be deemed consent. This review application was dismissed by Tribunal 5. Aforesaid judgment and orders were under challenge in this appeal. Appellant had challenged order invalidating him from service on medical grounds and had prayed for directions that he be promoted to post of Wing Commander and that names of his family members (wife and daughter) be recorded in service record and allow all benefits due to them.

Held, while allowing the appeal

1. It was a common ground that in terms of relevant policy, a serving officer would be required to obtain permission before any marriage with a foreign national could be contracted. On 27th August, 2008 Appellant applied to Directorate seeking permission to marry. According to relevant policy, document marriage could not be contracted without requisite permission to marry and in case no communication was received from Directorate for 120 days, there would be deemed consent and permission. Appellant without waiting for express permission or expiry of 120 days, did contract marriage on 19th December, 2008. Any violation on part of officer of mandate concerned policy could visit him with possibility of departmental action including dismissal or removal from service. [16]

2. In present case, neither there was any action taken against Appellant for infraction of mandatory requirement of policy nor re was any express communication rejecting his request seeking permission. As a matter of fact, there was no communication at all within 120 days. [17]

3. After having contracted marriage, Appellant also applied for ex-post facto permission for marriage. However, said application was not considered at all as, in meantime, Appellant was released from Indian Air Force and ceased to be governed by provisions of Indian Air Force Act, as asserted in counter affidavit. [18]

4. Underlying idea behind policy was that, in case a person governed by provisions of Indian Air Force Act, 1950 intended to contract marriage with a foreign national, requisite intimation in that behalf was required to be made and appropriate permission was also required to be obtained. As a part of exercise, foreign national with whom marriage was to be contracted may be required to give up original citizenship and acquire citizenship of India. If there be any infraction or violation of mandate of requirements, concerned officer could be visited with penalty including dismissal or removal from service. Policy had well laid and designed procedure including timelines and time limit of 120 days within which authorities were required to apply their mind and consider application seeking permission. In case nothing was heard within 120 days, policy incorporates concept of deemed consent or permission. [19]

5. Initial application was dated 27th October, 2008 and he was invalidated out of service with effect from 18th November, 2009 on medical grounds and not for any infraction of aforesaid policy. As a matter of fact, department did not respond for more than 120 days in matter. [20]

6. Policy in question was aimed at regulating certain aspects while officers were in service. If an officer after his release or retirement could, therefore, validly contract marriage with a foreign national and spouse would therefore be entitled to all benefits including medical or hospital facilities or club membership or canteen facilities etc., it did not stand to reason why Appellant, at least after his release from Indian Air Force, should be disentitled in that behalf. [21]

7. In facts and circumstances of case, Respondents were directed to include names of wife and daughter of Appellant in Service Certificate at least from date of his release or retirement and direct Respondents to extend to wife and daughter of Appellant all such benefits which a spouse and children of a retired officer would be entitled. [22]

8. Appeals allowed. [23]

Disposition:

Appeal Allowed

CHAPTER TEN

Vijaynath Jha vs. Union of India (UOI) and Ors. (18.05.2018 - SC) : MANU/SC/0593/2018

Relative Section:

Army Act, 1950 - Section 18, Army Act, 1950 - Section 27, Army Act, 1950 - Section 33; Armed Forces Tribunal Act 2007 - Section 2, Armed Forces Tribunal Act 2007 - Section 3; Navy Act, 1957 - Section 15(1); Air Force Act, 1950 - Section 18; Indian Stamp Act, 1899; Indian Tolls (Army and Air Force) Act, 1901 - Section 3; Pensions Act, 1871 - Section 11; Code of Civil Procedure, 1908 (CPC) - Section 60; Army Rules; Central Civil Services (Control, Classification and Appeal) Rules, 1965; Army Regulations; Constitution of India - Article 226

Hon'bleJudges/Coram:

A.K. Sikri and Ashok Bhushan, JJ.

Equivalent Citation: AIR2018SC2746, 2018(5) ALJ 126, [2018(159)FLR976], 2018/INSC/540, 2018LabIC3079, 2018(7) SCALE626, (2018)7SCC303, (2018)2SCC(LS)319, 2018 (5) SCJ 480, [2018]4SCR560, 2018(3)SCT4(SC)

Case Reference:

Brig. A.K. Bhutani v. Union of India; Union of India and Ors. v. Colonel G.S. Grewal MANU/SC/0517/2014 : 2014 (7) SCC 303;

Mohammed Ansari v. Union of India and Ors. MANU/SC/0106/2017 : 2017 (3) SCC 740;

Maj. General S.B. Akali Etc. Etc. v. Union of India and Ors. T.A. No. 125 of 2010

NumberofPagesintheOriginalJudgment:10

Case Note:

Service - Maintainability of Order - Section 33 of Army Act, 1950 - Present appeal filed challenging order whereby Armed Forces Tribunal (AFT) rejected Appellants application as not maintainable - Whether Appellant's application was maintainable before AFT

Facts:

The Appellant was commissioned in the Indian Army and his name was selected for permanent secondment in the Directorate General of Quality Assurance (DGQA). The Appellant was not found fit for permanent secondment. The Appellant filed a statutory complaint seeking permanent secondment, however the AFT rejected his application on grounds of maintainability. Hence, present appeal was filed.

Held, while dismissing the Appeal:

(i) The Appellant, had further relied on two provisions namely, Section 27 and Section 33 of the Army Act, 1950, Section 27 provides a remedy to aggrieved officers to submit a complaint to the Central Government, if he has been wronged by a commanding officer or any superior officer. Present was not a case where any action of commanding officer or any superior officer of Appellant was complained or questioned. Thus Section 27 had no application. Section 33 of the Act, provides for "saving of rights and privileges under other laws". The said provision indicates that the provision saves the rights and privileges conferred on persons subject to Army Act, by any other law for the time being in force." The above provision had no application in facts of the present case. Present was not a case where the Appellant was claiming any privilege conferred on persons subject to Army Act or by any other law in force. Section 33, thus, has no application. [24],[25],[26] and[27]

Disposition:

Appeal Dismissed

CHAPTER ELEVEN

Union of India (UOI) and Ors. vs. Shri Kant Sharma and Ors. (11.03.2015 - SC) : MANU/SC/0242/2015

Relative Section:

CONSTITUTION OF INDIA - Article 226; CONSTITUTION OF INDIA - Article 227; CONSTITUTION OF INDIA - Article 32; ARMED FORCES TRIBUNAL ACT 2007 - Section 30; ARMED FORCES TRIBUNAL ACT 2007 - Section 31;

Hon'bleJudges/Coram:

S.J. Mukhopadhaya and N.V. Ramana, JJ.

Equivalent Citation: 2015III AD (S.C.) 431, AIR2015SC2465, 2015(3)ESC515(SC), 2015/INSC/206, 2015LabIC2184, 2016(1)LLN14(SC), 2015-4- LW1, 2015(3)SCALE546, (2015)6SCC773, (2015)2SCC(LS)386, 2015 (3) SCJ 689, [2015]4SCR676, 2015(2)SCT519(SC), 2015(4)SLR610(SC)

Case Reference:

Ous Kutilingal Achudan Nair v. Union of India MANU/SC/0057/1975 : (1976) 2 SCC 780;

L. Chandra Kumar v. Union of India MANU/SC/0261/1997 : (1997) 3 SCC 261;

Kesavananda Bharati 1993 4 SCC 225; Indira Gandhi MANU/SC/0304/1975 : 1975 Supp SCC 1;

Minerva Mills MANU/SC/0075/1980 : (1980) 3 SCC 625;

S.N. Mukherjee v. Union of India MANU/SC/0346/1990 : (1990) 4 SCC 594;

R.K. Jain v. Union of India and Ors. MANU/SC/0291/1993 : (1993) 4 SCC 119;

S.P. Sampath Kumar v. Union of India;

M.B. Majumdar v. Union of India;

J.B. Chopra v. Union of India;

Babubhai Muljibhai Patel v. Nandlal Khodidas Barot and Ors. MANU/SC/0404/1974 : AIR 1974 SC 2105;

Gunwant Kaur v. Bhatinda Municipality MANU/SC/0397/1969 : AIR 1970 SC 802;

Mafatlal Industries Ltd. and Ors. v. Union of India and Ors. MANU/SC/1203/1997 : (1997) 5 SCC 536;

Kanaiyalal Lalchand and Sachdev and Ors. v. State of Maharashtra and Ors. MANU/SC/0103/2011 : (2011) 2 SCC 782;

Sadhana Lodh v. National Insurance Co. Ltd.;

Surya Dev Rai v. Ram Chander Rai;

SBI v. Allied Chemical Laboratories;

City and Industrial Development Corporation v. Dosu Aardeshir Bhiwandiwala;

Nivedita Sharma v. Cellular Operators Association of India and Ors. MANU/SC/1538/2011 : (2011) 14 SCC 337;

Wolverhampton New Waterworks Co. v. Hawkesford;

Neville v. London Express Newspapers Ltd.;

Attorney General of Trinidad and Tobago v. Gordon Grant and Co. Ltd.;

Secy. of State v. Mask and Co.;

Baburam Prakash Chandra Maheshwari v. Antarim Zila Parishad;

Thansingh Nathmal v. Supt. of Taxes 8 and Ors.;

Executive Engineer, Southern Electricity Supply Co. of Orissa Ltd. (SOUTHCO) and Anr. v. Sri Seetaram Rice Mill MANU/SC/1334/2011 : (2012) 2 SCC 108;

Cicily Kallarackal v. Vehicle Factory MANU/SC/0672/2012 : 2012 (8) SCC 524;

Commissioner of Income Tax and Ors. v. Chhabil Dass Agrawal MANU/SC/0802/2013 : (2014) 1 SCC 603;

Harbanslal Sahnia v. Indian Oil Corporation Ltd.;

State of H.P. v. Gujarat Ambuja Cement Ltd.;

K.S. Rashid and Son v. Income Tax Investigation Commission;

Sangram Singh v. Election Tribunal;

Union of India v. T.R. Varma; State of U.P. v. Mohd. Nooh;

K.S. Venkataraman and Co. (P) Ltd. v. State of Madras;

N.T. Veluswami Thevar v. G. Raja Nainar; Municipal Council, Khurai v. Kamal Kumar;

Siliguri Municipality v. Amalendu Das; S.T. Muthusami v. K. Natarajan;

Rajasthan SRTC v. Krishna Kant; Kerala SEB v. Kurien E. Kalathil;

A. Venkatasubbiah Naidu v. S. Chellappan;

L.L. Sudhakar Reddy v. State of A.P.;

Shri Sant Sadguru Janardan Swami (Moingiri Maharaj) Sahakari Dugdha Utpadak Sanstha v. State of Maharashtra;

Pratap Singh v. State of Haryana; GKN Driveshafts (India) Ltd. v. ITO;

G. Veerappa Pillai v. Raman and Raman Ltd.; CCE v. Dunlop India Ltd.;

Ramendra Kishore Biswas v. State of Tripura;

Shivgonda Anna Patil v. State of Maharashtra;

C.A. Abraham v. ITO;

Titaghur Paper Mills Co. Ltd. v. State of Orissa;

Excise and Taxation Officer-cum-Assessing Authority v. Gopi Nath and Sons;

Whirlpool Corporation v. Registrar of Trade Marks;

Tin Plate Co. of India Ltd. v. State of Bihar;

Sheela Devi v. Jaspal Singh;

Punjab National Bank v. O.C. Krishnan;

Union of India v. Brigadier P.S. Gill MANU/SC/0234/2012 : (2012) 4 SCC 463

NumberofPagesintheOriginalJudgment: 25

Case Note:

Defence - Right of Appeal - Sections 30 and 31 of Armed Forces Tribunal Act, 2007 - High Court entertained writ petitions filed under Article 226 of Constitution against well considered and reasoned order passed by Tribunal - Hence, present appeal - Whether right of appeal under Section 30 of Act, 2007, against order of Armed Forces Tribunal with leave of Tribunal Under Section 31 of Act or leave granted by Supreme Court, or bar of leave to appeal before Supreme Court Under Article 136(2) of Constitution of India, will bar jurisdiction of High Court Under Article 226 of Constitution of India regarding matters related to Armed Forces - Held, there is constitutional bar not only Under Article 136(2) but also Under Article 227(4) of Constitution of India with regard to entertaining any determination or order passed by any court or Tribunal under law relating to Armed Forces - Any legislation including Armed Forces Act, 2007 cannot override or curtail jurisdiction of High Court Under Article 226 of Constitution of India - Though Under Section 30 no person has right of appeal against final order or decision of Tribunal to this Court other than those falling Under Section 30(2) of Act, but it is statutory appeal which lies to this Court - High Court while entertaining writ petition under Article 226 of Constitution bypassed machinery created under Sections 30 and 31 of Act - Therefore, High Court was not justified in entertaining petition Under Article 226 of Constitution of India - Impugned judgments passed by Delhi High Court was set aside - Appeal disposed of. [paras 19, 25, 33, 37 and 38]

Facts:

1. In these appeals the question raised is whether the right of appeal Under Section 30 of the Armed Forces Tribunal Act, 2007 (hereinafter referred to as the 'Act'), against an order of Armed Forces Tribunal (hereinafter referred to as the 'Tribunal') with the leave of the Tribunal Under Section 31 of the Act or leave granted by the Supreme Court, or bar of leave to appeal before the Supreme Court Under Article 136(2) of the Constitution of India, will bar the jurisdiction of the High Court Under Article 226 of the Constitution of India regarding matters related to Armed Forces.

Union of India and Ors. are the Appellants in all these appeals except in C.A. No. 7338, C.A. No. 7399 of 2013 and C.A. No. 96/2014 wherein they are the Respondents. The Respondents in all these appeals except the three mentioned above are-Army Personnel who moved before the Tribunal for adjudication or trial of disputes and complaints with respect to condition of service. Having not granted relief, the Army personnel assailed the order passed by the Tribunal before the respective High Courts Under Article 226 of the Constitution. The Appellant in C.A. No. 7338 of 2013 on being aggrieved by the order passed by the Armed Forces Tribunal, Regional Bench, Chennai challenged the same before the High Court of Judicature of Andhra Pradesh at Hyderabad. In the cases in hand except C.A. No. 7338 of 2013 and C.A. No. 96 of 2014 the High Court entertained the writ petitions and adjudicated the disputes. The High Court having granted relief after reversing the order of Tribunal, the Union of India has challenged the same. In C.A. No. 7338 of 2013 and C.A. No. 96 of 2014, the Appellants-Army Personnel have challenged the orders by which High Courts refused to entertain their writ petitions. In C.A. No. 7399 of 2013, the Appellant-

Army Personnel has challenged the order of Delhi High Court allowing the writ petition of Respondent No. 2 therein.

2. At the outset, in all the writ petitions preliminary objection was raised on behalf of the Union of India as to the maintainability of the writ petition on the ground that against the orders impugned a remedy of appeal to the Supreme Court is provided Under Section 30 of the Armed Forces Tribunal Act, 2007.

3. Learned Counsel appearing on behalf of the Union of India submitted that the High Court cannot entertain writ petitions Under Article 226 of the Constitution of India contrary to the law enacted by the Parliament being the Armed Forces Tribunal, 2007 which is a special enactment exclusively provided for an appellate remedy by way of leave before this Court.

Further, according to learned Counsel for the Union of India as none of the Respondents raised any issue of jurisdiction of the Tribunal and it was essentially a challenge to the order of the Armed Forces Tribunal only on merits. Therefore, the High Court was not correct in entertaining the writ petitions Under Article 226 of the Constitution against the well considered and reasoned order passed by the Tribunal.

Held by Hon'ble Supreme Court

If the High Court entertains a petition Under Article 226 of the Constitution of India against order passed by Armed Forces Tribunal Under Section 14 or Section 15 of the Act bypassing the machinery of statute i.e. Sections 30 and 31 of the Act, there is likelihood of anomalous situation for the aggrieved person in praying for relief from this Court.

Section 30 provides for an appeal to this Court subject to leave granted Under Section 31 of the Act. By Clause (2) of Article 136 of the Constitution of India, the appellate jurisdiction of this Court Under Article 136 has been excluded in relation to any judgment, determination, sentence or order passed or made by any court or Tribunal constituted by or under any law relating to the Armed Forces. If any person aggrieved by the order of the Tribunal, moves before the High Court Under Article 226 and the High Court entertains the petition and passes a judgment or order, the person who may be aggrieved against both the orders passed by the Armed Forces Tribunal and the High Court, cannot challenge both the orders in one joint appeal. The aggrieved person may file leave to appeal Under Article 136 of the Constitution against the judgment passed by the High Court but in view of the bar of jurisdiction by Clause (2) of Article 136, this Court cannot entertain appeal against the order of the Armed Forces

Tribunal. Once, the High Court entertains a petition Under Article 226 of the Constitution against the order of Armed Forces Tribunal and decides the matter, the person who thus approached the High Court, will also be precluded from filing an appeal Under Section 30 with leave to appeal Under Section 31 of the Act against the order of the Armed Forces Tribunal as he cannot challenge the order passed by the High Court Under Article 226 of the Constitution Under Section 30 read with Section 31 of the Act. Thereby, there is a chance of anomalous situation. Therefore, it is always desirable for the High Court to act in terms of the law laid down by this Court as referred to above, which is binding on the High Court Under Article 141 of the Constitution of India, allowing the aggrieved person to avail the remedy Under Section 30 read with Section 31 Armed Forces Act.

38. The High Court (Delhi High Court) while entertaining the writ petition Under Article 226 of the Constitution bypassed the machinery created Under Sections 30 and 31 of Act. However, we find that Andhra Pradesh High Court and the Allahabad High Court had not entertained the petitions Under Article 226 and directed the writ Petitioners to seek resort Under Sections 30 and 31 of the Act. Further, the law laid down by this Court, as referred to above, being binding on the High Court, we are of the view that Delhi High Court was not justified in entertaining the petition Under Article 226 of the Constitution of India.

39. For the reasons aforesaid, we set aside the impugned judgments passed by the Delhi High Court and upheld the judgments and orders passed by the Andhra Pradesh High Court and Allahabad High Court. Aggrieved persons are given liberty to avail the remedy Under Section 30 with leave to appeal Under Section 31 of the Act, and if so necessary may file petition for condonation of delay to avail remedy before this Court.

40. The Civil Appeal Nos. 7400, 7375-7376, 7399, 9388, 9389 of 2013 are allowed and the Civil Appeal Nos. 7338 of 2013 and 96 of 2014 are dismissed.

CHAPTER TWELVE

Union of India (UOI) and Ors. vs. Parashotam Dass (21.03.2023 - SC) : MANU/SC/0285/2023

Relative Section:

ARMED FORCES TRIBUNAL ACT 2007 - Section 3; ARMED FORCES TRIBUNAL ACT 2007 - Section 14; CONSTITUTION OF INDIA - Article 226, CONSTITUTION OF INDIA - Article 227.

Hon'bleJudges/Coram:

Sanjay Kishan Kaul, Abhay Shreeniwas Oka and B.V. Nagarathna, JJ.

Equivalent Citation: 2023/INSC/264, (2023)2MLJ653

Case Reference:

Prithi Pal Singh Bedi and Ors. v. Union of India (UOI) and Ors. MANU/SC/0233/1982;

L. Chandra Kumar v. Union of India (UOI) and Ors. MANU/SC/0261/1997;

Kesavananda Bharati Sripadagalvaru v. State of Kerala MANU/SC/0445/1973;

S.N. Mukherjee v. Union of India (UOI) MANU/SC/0346/1990;

Union of India (UOI) and Ors. v. Shri Kant Sharma and Ors. MANU/SC/0242/2015;

Rojer Mathew v. South Indian Bank Ltd. and Ors. MANU/SC/1563/2019;

Daxina Kumari v. Union of India SLP(C) No. 20721/2015;

K.C. Shibu v. Union of India SLP(C) No. 17320/2017;

Krishna Nandan Mishra v. Union of India SLP(C) No. 20499/2015;
Nand Lal Verma v. Union of India SLP(C) No. 26617/2015;
Randeep Singh Guleria v. Union of India SLP(C) No. 26568/2015;
Gopi Ram v. Union of India SLP(C) No. 26620/2015;
Avi Chander Sud v. Union of India SLP(C) No. 36386/2015;
Gurcharan Singh v. Union of India SLP(C) No. 5111/2016;
Nirmal Singh v. Union of India SLP (C) No. 28101/2016;
Davinder Singh v. Union of India SLP(C) No. 1788/2023;
Union of India v. Parashotam Dass SLP(C) No. 34797/2014;
Union of India v. Thomas Vaidyan M. Civil Appeal No. 5327/2015;
Gurbux Singh Dhindsa v. Union of India WP(C) No. 76/2016

NumberofPagesintheOriginalJudgment:12

Case Note:

Defence - Writ jurisdiction - Armed forces tribunal- Articles 226, 227, 323A and 323B of Constitution of India - Present petition filed with regard toexercise of jurisdiction under Article 226 of Constitution of India by High Court in order passed by Armed Forces Tribunal - It was submitted that exclusion of judicial review under Article 226 of Constitution ought not to be countenanced because of lack of any viable alternative appeal mechanism - Whether order passed by Armed Forces Tribunal would be amenable to challenge in writ jurisdiction under Article 226 of Constitution of India before any High Court.

Facts:

The present petition filed with regard to exercise of jurisdiction under Article 226 of Constitution of India by High Court in order passed by Armed Forces Tribunal. It was strongly contended that there could never be a bar to the exercise of jurisdiction under Article 226 of the Constitution of India by the High Court, albeit, sometimes, the High Court makes its discretion not to exercise its jurisdiction. It was further submitted that the exclusion of judicial review review under Article 226 of the Constitution ought not to be countenanced because of lack of any viable alternative appeal mechanism.

Held, while disposing off the petition:

(i) This court was unable to appreciate the observations in the case of Major General Shri Kant Sharma and Anr., which sought to put an embargo on the exercise of jurisdiction under Article 226 of the Constitution, diluting a very significant provision of the Constitution which also forms the part of basic structure. The principles of basic structure have withstood the test of time and were emphasized in many judicial pronouncements as an ultimate test. This was not something that could be doubted. That being the position, the self-restraint of the High Court under Article 226 of the Constitution was distinct from putting an embargo on the High Court in exercising this jurisdiction under Article 226 of the Constitution while judicially reviewing a decision arising from an order of the Tribunal. [25]

(ii) On the legislature introducing the concept of Tribunalisation, the same was tested in L. Chandra Kumar case before a Bench of seven Judges of this Court. Thus, while upholding the principles of Tribunalisationunder Article 323A or Article 323B, the Bench was unequivocally of the view that decisions of Tribunals would be subject to the jurisdiction of the High Court under Article 226of the Constitution, and would not be restricted by the forty second Constitutional Amendment which introduced the said two Articles. This should have put the matter to rest, and no Bench of less than seven Judges could have doubted the proposition. The need for the observations in the five-Judges' Bench in Rojer Mathewcase qua the Armed Forces Tribunal really arose because of the observations made in Major General Shri Kant Sharma and Anr. Thus, it was, reiterated and clarified that the power of the High Court under Article 226 of the Constitution was not inhibited, and superintendence and control under Article 227 of the Constitution were somewhat distinct from the powers of judicial review under Article 226 of the Constitution. [26]

(iii) There was no necessity to carve out certain cases from the scope of judicial review under Article 226 of the Constitution. It was enunciated in the Constitution Bench judgment in S.N. Mukherjee case that even in respect of courts-martial, the High Court could grant appropriate relief in a certain scenario as envisaged therein, i.e., if the said proceedings have resulted in denial of the fundamental rights guaranteed under Part III of the Constitution or if the said proceedings suffer from a jurisdictional error or any error of law apparent on the face of the record. [29]

Disposition:

Disposed of

CHAPTER THIRTEEN

Balkrishna Ram vs. Union of India (UOI) and Ors. (09.01.2020 - SC) : MANU/SC/0021/2020

Relative Section:

Allahabad High Court Rules, 1952 - Rule 5; Armed Forces Tribunal Act 2007 - Section 5(6), Section 14(1), Section 14(2), Section 15, Section 28, Section 34, Section 34(1); Constitution of India - Article 14, Article 15, Article 16, Article 32, Article 136, Article 214, Article 215, Article 226,Article 227,Article 323A,Article 323B; Uttar Pradesh High Court (Abolition of Letters Patent Appeals) Act, 1962.

Hon'bleJudges/Coram:

Deepak Gupta and Aniruddha Bose, JJ.

Equivalent Citation:AIR2020SC341, 129(2020)CLT703, 2020(1)ESC91(SC), 2020/INSC/26, (2020) 197 PLR404 , (2020)2SCC442, (2020)1SCC(LS)351, [2020]2SCR581, 2020(1)SCT576(SC), 2020(1)SLJ365(SC), 2020(4)SLR488(SC)

Cases Referred:

Union of India (UOI) and Ors. v. Shri Kant Sharma and Ors. MANU/SC/0242/2015;

L. Chandra Kumar v. Union of India and others MANU/SC/0261/1997;

W.Ex. Sigman Nand Kishore Sahoo v. Chief of Army Staff and Ors. MANU/UP/1142/2011;

Union of India (UOI) v. T.R. Varma MANU/SC/0121/1957;

Union of India and Ors. v. Ram Baran Special Appeal Defective No. 445 of 2005;

Rojer Mathew v. South Indian Bank Ltd. and Ors. MANU/SC/1563/2019

NumberofPagesintheOriginalJudgment:10

Case Note:

Defence - Appeal - Jurisdiction to entertain - Sections 14(1) and 34 of Armed Forces Tribunal Act, 2007 - Present appeal filed to determine jurisdiction with regard to appeal against order of Single judge of High Court deciding case related to Armed Forces personnel pending before High Court - Whether appeal against order of Single judge of High Court deciding case related to Armed Forces personnel pending before High Court was required to be transferred to Armed Forces Tribunal or should be heard by High Court.

Facts:

The present appeal had been filed to determine jurisdiction with regard to appeal against an order of a single judge of a High Court deciding a case related to an Armed Forces personnel pending before the High Court. It was contending by the Appellant that the AFT exercises all the powers of the High Court. She submits that it virtually substitutes the High Court in so far as matters governed by the Act were concerned, and as such an LPA or Special Appeal against the judgment of a single judge was also required to be transferred to the AFT.

Held, while disposing off the appeal:

(i) Section 14(1) of the Act clearly provides that the AFT will exercise powers of all courts except the Supreme Court or High Court exercising jurisdiction under Article 226 and 227 of the Constitution of India. Section 34 is very carefully worded. It states that every suit, or other proceedings pending before any court including a High Court immediately before the establishment of the Tribunal shall stand transferred on that day to the Tribunal. The Legislature had clearly not vested the AFT with the power and jurisdiction of the High Court to be exercised under Article 226 of the Constitution. The High Court could exercise its writ jurisdiction even in respect of orders passed by the AFT. True it was, that since an appeal lies to the Supreme Court against an order of the AFT, the High Court may not exercise their extraordinary writ jurisdiction because there was an efficacious alternative remedy available but that did not mean that the jurisdiction of the High Court was taken away. In a given circumstance, the High Court may and can exercise its extraordinary writ jurisdiction even against the orders of the High Court. [10]

(ii) The High Court is a Constitutional Court constituted under Article 214 of the Constitution and are courts of record within the meaning of Article 215. It was obvious that the order of the High Court could not be challenged before any other forum except the Supreme Court. The provision of intra-court appeal whether by way of Letters Patents or special enactment is a system that provides for correction of judgments within the High Courts where a judgment rendered by a single judge may be subject to challenge before a Division Bench. This appeal to the Division Bench does not lie in all cases and must be provided for either under the Letters Patent or any other special enactment. Even where such appeal lies the appeal was heard by two or more judges of the High Court. This court could nnot envisage a situation where an appeal against the order of a sitting judge of the High Court was heard by a Tribunal comprising of one retired judge and one retired Armed Forces official. Therefore, reject the contention that an intra court appeal from the judgment of a single judge of the High Court to a Division Bench pending in the High Court was required to be transferred under Section 34 of the Act. [17]

(iii) It was not necessary to indicate in the order of discharge whether such consideration took place or not. From the records of the case, it was found that before discharge, the name of the Appellant was considered for two categories but unfortunately the Appellant could not meet the height criteria for appointment to either of the posts. Thus, this clearly shows that his case was considered as per the extant policy but he was not fit for appointment. [19]

Disposition:

Appeal Dismissed

CHAPTER FOURTEEN

Om Prakash vs. Union of India (UOI) and Ors. (09.07.2015 - SC) : MANU/SC/0762/2015

Relative Section:

Army Act, 1950 - Section 164, Army Act, 1950 - Section 164(2); Armed Forces Tribunal Act 2007 - Section 15; Indian Penal Code, 1860 (IPC) - Section 302, Indian Penal Code, 1860 (IPC) - Section 304; Army Rules, 1954 - Rule 23, Army Rules, 1954 - Rule 23(1), Army Rules, 1954 - Rule 23(2), Army Rules, 1954 - Rule 23(3), Army Rules, 1954 - Rule 23(4), Army Rules, 1954 - Rule 23(6)

Hon'bleJudges/Coram:

Dipak Misra and N.V. Ramana

Equivalent Citation: 2015(3)ACR2620, 2015IX AD (S.C.) 99, 2015(152)AIC200, 2015(3)AJR850, 2015 (2) ALD(Crl.) 811 (SC), 2015 (91) ACC 316, 2015(4)BLJ27, III(2015)CCR272(SC), 2015CriLJ3796, 2015(4)Crimes402(SC), 2015(3)ECrN502, 2015/INSC/491, 2015(4)JCC2489(SC), (2015) 3 MLJ(Crl) 632 (SC), 2016(1)N.C.C.123, 2015(3)RCR(Criminal)993, 2015(7)SCALE655, (2015)8SCC705, 2015 (6) SCJ 696, [2015]8SCR467, 2015(3)UC2157

Case Reference:

Gilbert Pereira v. State of Karntaka MANU/SC/0662/2004 : AIR 2004 12 SCC 281;

Ravindran v. Superintendent of Customs MANU/SC/7649/2007 : (2007) 6 SCC 410;

Rumi Bora Dutta v. State of Assam MANU/SC/0593/2013 : (2013) 7 SCC 417;

Hema v. State MANU/SC/0017/2013 : (2013) 10 SCC 192;

Union of India v. Major Rabinder Singh MANU/SC/1140/2011 : (2012) 12 SCC 787;

Appabhai v. State of Gujarat MANU/SC/0028/1988 : AIR 1988 SC 696;

Rohtash Kumar v. State of Haryana MANU/SC/0573/2013 : (2013) 14 SCC 434;

Bachan Singh v. Union of India and Ors. MANU/SC/7791/2008 : (2008) 9 SCC 161

NumberofPagesintheOriginalJudgment:9

Case Note:

Criminal - Culpable homicide not amounting to murder - Section 304 Indian Penal Code, 1860 - Appellant was member of the armed forces - Appellant stabbed deceased during altercation - Surrendered at police station - Gave confessional statement before police and regiment officers - Whether on the facts adduced the prosecution has proved its case against the Appellant

Facts

The Appellant and the deceased had an altercation in the barracks, during which the Appellant stabbed the deceased. Subsequently, the Appellant surrendered at the police station and stated that he had stabbed one person with a knife. He made a confessional statement before the police and army officers.

The General Court Martial relied on the confessional statement of the Appellant, statements of members of the regiment describing the events that lead up to the altercation and statements of those witness to the Appellant's confession. The doctor's report stated that the stab wound was sufficient in the ordinary course to cause death. The General Court Martial found the Appellant guilty, which was upheld by the Armed Forces Tribunal.

Hence, the present appeal. The Appellant contends that the evidence cannot form the foundation of conviction. The confession made by the Appellant at the police station in presence of the authorities cannot be taken into consideration. The Tribunal relied upon hearsay evidence, which make the analysis perverse. The knife used to cause the injury has not been recovered.

Held, dismissing the appeal

1. The Appellant had an altercation prior to the stabbing as well. The Appellant was in a drunken state and he alone was present in the room. His presence at the police station at an odd hour and his absence at the "fall in parade", clearly establish the guilt of the accused. The minor discrepancies do not dent the testimony of the prosecution witnesses to treat them as reproachable and do not destroy the prosecution version.[12]

2.A warning was given to the Appellant that whatever he would say would be taken down in writing and given in evidence. There was no compulsion. The Appellant's statement has been proven before the GCM. Nothing has been elicited in the cross-examination or brought on record which will make the confessional statement hollow and unreliable. The appeal stands dismissed.[16] and[17]

CHAPTER FIFTEEN

Union of India (UOI) and Ors. vs. Kuldeep Yadav (25.09.2019 - SC) : MANU/SC/1320/2019

Relative Section:

Armed Forces Tribunal Act 2007 - Section 14(5)

Hon'bleJudges/Coram:

A.M. Khanwilkar and Ajay Rastogi

Equivalent Citation: 2019(5)ALT404, 2019(4)ESC879(SC), 2019/INSC/1083, (2019)7MLJ428, 2019(13)SCALE46, (2019)10SCC449, (2020)1SCC(LS)110, [2019]15SCR662, 2019(4)SCT481(SC), 2019(3)SLJ255(SC), 2020(1)SLR646(SC)

Case Reference:

Ranjit Thakur v. Union of India (UOI) and Ors. MANU/SC/0691/1987;

B.C. Chaturvedi v. Union of India and others MANU/SC/0118/1996;

Union of India (UOI) and Ors. v. Bodupalli Gopalaswami MANU/SC/1067/2011;

Union of India (UOI) v. Parma Nand MANU/SC/0636/1989;

Mithilesh Singh v. Union of India (UOI) and Ors. MANU/SC/0160/2003;

General Court Martial and Ors. v. Col. Aniltej Singh Dhaliwal MANU/SC/0902/1998;

Union of India (UOI) and Ors. v. Dwarka Prasad Tiwari MANU/SC/4513/2006;

S.R. Tewari v. Union of India (UOI) and Anr. MANU/SC/0566/2013

NumberofPagesintheOriginalJudgment:150

Case Note:

Service - Punishment of censure -Challenge in present case was regarding interference with awarding of Severe Displeasure (Recordable) by disciplinary authority - Whether Armed Forces Tribunal despite noting that, punishment of censure awarded by competent authority could not be faulted, ought to have interfered on specious ground that, "Severe Displeasure (Recordable)" was not commensurate and excessive in facts of present case; and to direct competent authority to award censure other than "Severe Displeasure (Recordable)", merely because censure could also be of Severe Displeasure (Non-Recordable) or mere Displeasure, as case might - Whether this approach, inevitably, entailed in sitting over subjective satisfaction of competent authority in matter of awarding punishment.

Facts:

The limited challenge is regarding the interference with the awarding of Severe Displeasure (Recordable) by the disciplinary authority. That has been done despite a categorical finding that the fact situation of this case warrants a censure against the Respondent, for having violated the above stated Instructions. It is urged that the quantum and nature of punishment is the sole prerogative of the disciplinary authority; and in the present case, that discretion has been exercised with due consideration of all the relevant matters. It is urged that the punishment awarded to the Respondent by no standards can be labelled as shockingly disproportionate. However, the Tribunal got swayed away on tenuous reasoning; and interfered with a just decision of the appropriate authorities. It is urged by the Appellant that brilliant service record of the Respondent cannot wash away the indiscretion which could have escalated to threats concerning national security. Further, the authorities were fully conscious about the service record of the Respondent and after duly considering all aspects decided to award Severe Displeasure (Recordable). The acts of commission and omission of the Respondent, which, he admitted to have indulged in, were inexcusable and warranted a serious departmental action. Indisputably, the Respondent had admitted to have remained in touch with a foreign national for over two years including having facilitated her to visit India and also stayed with her in the Army officers' mess guest room by making false entries in the respective diary and giving false identity that foreign national was his wife. The lesser action of censure of Severe Displeasure (Recordable), therefore, by no standards can be said to be untenable on facts or in law.

Held, while allowing the appeal

1. It is no more res integra that the Tribunal is competent and empowered to interfere with the punishment awarded by the appropriate authority in any departmental action, on the ground that the same is excessive or disproportionate to the misconduct proved against the delinquent officer. However, exercise of that power is circumscribed. It can be invoked only in exceptional and rare cases, when the punishment awarded by the disciplinary authority shocks the conscience of the Tribunal or is so unreasonable that no reasonable person would have taken such an action. The Tribunal, ordinarily, is not expected to examine the quantum and nature of punishment awarded by the disciplinary authority as a court of appeal and substitute its own view and findings by replacing the subjective satisfaction arrived at by the competent authority in the backdrop of the evidence on record. [22]

2. Indeed, it is open to the Tribunal to direct the disciplinary authority to reconsider the penalty imposed by it; and in exceptional and rare cases, may itself impose appropriate punishment to shorten the litigation by recording cogent reasons therefor. The reported decisions pressed into service by the Appellants have consistently taken this view. In the present case, the Tribunal has adopted the former option, of relegating the Respondent before the competent authority for reconsideration of the punishment but, at the same time, hedged by an observation that awarding of censure in the facts of the present case was inevitable. [23]

3. Indeed, the past service records of the delinquent officer may be germane for awarding punishment. But in the present case, the same had been duly noticed by the competent authority as also by the authority considering the statutory complaint filed by the Respondent. [25]

4. The Tribunal also erroneously assumed that the competent authority opted to resort to administrative action by awarding censure instead of Court Martial, because it had condoned the misconduct of Respondent being of a minor nature and not being a case involving moral turpitude, fraud, theft, dishonesty and misappropriation. This basis is plainly misdirected and not in conformity with the applicable policy regarding award of censure to Officers and JCO's circulated vide communication dated 23rd April, 2007. In fact, the Tribunal has extracted the relevant portion of the said policy, which clearly predicates that in cases, which are not of a minor nature and not an act involving moral turpitude, fraud, theft,

dishonesty, financial irregularities or misappropriation where trial by a Court Martial is not practicable or is inexpedient due to other reasons, may if found appropriate, be forwarded to Integrated HQ of MoD (Army) (DV Dte.) at the discretion of the GOC-in-C for consideration of the award of censure by the COAS/Government. The case of the Respondent would certainly fall within the purview of the said clause. Indubitably, just because the competent authority chose to dispense with the disciplinary action of Court Martial qua the Respondent, does not make the misconduct and misdemeanour of the Respondent any less serious much less to be of a minor nature as assumed by the Tribunal. Notably, the Tribunal has taken such erroneous approach despite having noticed that the Respondent had admitted all the allegations made against him in the show cause notice. [26]

5. The Tribunal also committed a palpable error in opining that the show cause notice does not contain allegation against the Respondent, regarding furnishing wrong information in the guest list of the Army Guest House. The show cause notice vividly describes the serious lapses committed by the Respondent such as in Clause 2(a) (iv), namely, "unauthorisedly" bringing and staying with Ms. Sueli, a foreign national, in the Army premises in Goa from 12th October, 2011 to 15th October, 2011. This allegation was sufficient to include the misdemeanour of the Respondent of having furnished wrong information in the guest list of the guest house. This allegation has been admitted by the Respondent. [28]

6. The Tribunal also got swayed away by the fact that the allegation made in the show cause notice did not mention about "classified" documents on the laptop. It was of the view that only if reference was to be made to "classified" documents, it would have been a case of sensitive nature touching upon the security of the nation. What has been glossed over by the Tribunal, is that, the allegation against the Respondent in the show cause notice is about unauthorisedly keeping "official" documents in his laptop including the crucial information regarding his rank, name and unit location, and further the laptop containing such official documents/ information was routinely connected to the internet and made easily accessible to a foreign national. This allegation has been admitted by the Respondent in his response to the show cause notice. The Respondent merely wanted the competent authority to take a lenient view, being momentary loss of indiscretion. [29]

7. The Tribunal then adverted to the fact that the award of censure coincided with all the three chances of No. 3 Selection Board. That may be

the effect of censure on promotion. As per the Censure Policy, the intended punishment being permissible and the competent authority being satisfied that the same is commensurate with the seriousness of the uncontroverted allegations against the Respondent, for the reasons recorded in that regard by it, such satisfaction cannot be lightly brushed aside as being excessive or unjust. Accordingly, even this reason weighed with the Tribunal is unstatable and tenuous. [30]

8. Tribunal committed manifest error in interfering with the award of censure of Severe Displeasure (Recordable), in the facts of this case. The basis on which the Tribunal chose to interfere being indefensible, the conclusion reached by the Tribunal on such edifice must fall to the ground. [31]

9. In the backdrop of the uncontroverted allegations, as articulated in the show cause notice issued to the Respondent, reproduced in paragraph No. 5 hitherto, the same may warrant a stern action against the Respondent; and, thus, the discretion exercised by the competent authority in terms of the stated policy to deal with the Respondent administratively cannot be faulted with and must be upheld, including the award of censure of Severe Displeasure (Recordable) being commensurate thereto. [32]

10. Once, the Respondent chose not to controvert the allegations made against him in the show cause notice and pursued the matter with the competent authority only for taking a lenient view, he cannot be permitted to resile from that position. It would result in allowing the Respondent to approbate and reprobate. That cannot be countenanced. Therefore, the prayer of the Respondent to permit him to challenge the adverse findings of the Tribunal qua him on merits of the admitted allegations, is declined. [33]

11. The impugned judgment and order of the Armed Forces Tribunal is quashed and set aside. Instead, the decision of the Government of India dated 30th April, 2014, rejecting the statutory complaint of the Respondent and upholding the order passed by the GOC-in-C dated 10th May, 2013 is restored. [34]

12. Appeal is allowed. [35]

CHAPTER SIXTEEN

Kanhaiya Kumar vs. Union of India (UOI) and Ors. (09.01.2018 - SC) : MANU/SC/0172/2018

Relative Section:

Army Act, 1950 - Section 20,Section 20(1),Section 20(3), Section 37, Section 122, Section 122(1), Section 122(4); Armed Forces Tribunal Act 2007 - Section 14; Army Rules, 1954 - Rule 17; Central Civil Services (Pension) Rules - Rule 24

Hon'bleJudges/Coram:

A.K. Sikri and Ashok Bhushan,

Equivalent Citation: AIR2018SC2378, 2018 (3) CCC 314 , [2018(157)FLR765], 2018/INSC/13, 2018LabIC2574, 2018(3)SCALE312, (2018)14SCC279, (2018)2SCC(LS)664, [2018]1SCR679, 2018(2)SCT434(SC), 2018(3)SLR900(SC)

Case Reference:

Union of India and Ors. v. M. Bhaskaran MANU/SC/0178/1996 : 1995 Supp. (4) SCC 100;

Vice-chairman, Kendriya Vidyalaya Sangathan and Anr. v. Girdharilal Yadav MANU/SC/1303/2004 : (2004) 6 SCC 325;

Ram Saran v. IG of Police, CRPF and Ors. MANU/SC/0803/2006 : (2006) 2 SCC 541;

Associated Provincial Picture Houses Ltd. v. Wednesbury Corporation MANU/UKWA/0002/1947 : (1948) 1 KB 223 : (1947) 2 All ER 680 (CA);

V. Ramana v. A.P. SRTC MANU/SC/0539/2005 : (2005) 7 SCC 338: 2006 SCC (L&S) 69;

R. Vishwanatha Pillai v. State of Kerala MANU/SC/0023/2004 : (2004) 2 SCC 105: 2004 SCC (L&S) 350;

Rajeshwar Baburao Bone v. State of Maharashtra and Anr. MANU/SC/0807/2015 : (2015) 14 SCC 497;

Union of India and Ors. v. Major General Madan Lal Yadav (Retd.) MANU/SC/0355/1996 : (1996) 4 SCC 127;

Rajeshwar Baburao Bone v. State of Maharashtra WP No. 5160 of 2012

NumberofPagesintheOriginalJudgment:7

Case Note:

Service - Dismissal - Challenged thereof - Present appeal filed challenging order whereby Armed Forces Tribunal (AFT) dismissed Appellant from service on ground of fraudulent enrolment - Whether dismissal of Appellant justifiable

Facts:

The Appellant was enrolled in the Army and after few years of service a show cause notice was issued alleging offence of fraudulent enrolment based on a fake relationship certificate. The Appellants representation was not considered. The Appellant challenged the order whereby the AFT without admitting the formal original application, directed the Respondent to produce the relevant documents. Thereupon in reply, the Appellant had specifically admitted the fact that his father was not an Ex-serviceman and had produced and relied on a fake relationship certificate. Thus the AFT dismissed the Appellant from service. Hence, present appeal was filed.

Held, while dismissing appeal:

(i) The power of dismissal or removal could be exercised if the delinquent was informed of the particulars of the cause of action and allowed reasonable time to state in writing any reasons he may have to urge against his dismissal or removal from service. In the present case, such an opportunity was given to the Appellant. Gravamen of the charge is that he had got the enrolment on the basis of a fake relationship certificate. It was pertinent that in reply he admitted the fact that the relationship certificate produced by him was fake. Thus, the procedure was substantially followed. It was also an admitted position that but for the said fake relationship certificate, the Appellant could not have got enrolment in the Army. Thus, he got enrolment by playing a fraud. The fraud vitiates the entire action and in such a case the enrolment obtained by the Appellant, which was fraudulent. The argument of the Appellant that there should have been an inquiry into the matter was totally untenable when the Appellant himself had admitted that relationship certificate was fake, the procedure would be an empty formality. [9],[10] and[14]

Disposition:

Appeal Dismissed

CHAPTER SEVENTEEN

S. Muthu Kumaran vs. Union of India (UOI) and Ors. (17.01.2017 - SC) : MANU/SC/0062/2017

Relative Section:

Armed Forces Tribunal Act 2007 - Section 14,Section 30, Section 31; Army Act, 1950 - Section 20, Army Act, 1950 - Section 20(3); Army Rules, 1954 - Rule 17

Hon'bleJudges/Coram:

Dipak Misra and R. Banumathi, JJ.

Equivalent Citation: 2017 (1) CCC 83 , 2017(2)CLJ(SC)187, 2017(3)ESC438(SC), [2017(153) FLR613], 2017(1)SCALE564, (2017)4SCC609, (2017)2SCC(LS)123, [2017]1SCR550, 2017(2)SCT9(SC), 2017(3)SLR294(SC)

Case Reference: nil

NumberofPagesintheOriginalJudgment: 4

Case Note:

Service - Termination - Validity of punishment - Tribunal dismissed application filed by Appellant seeking reinstatement in service with all consequential benefits - Hence, present appeal - Whether termination of Appellant was justified

Facts:

The Appellant was alleged to have been involved in fraudulent recruitment racket and obtaining illegal gratification in lieu of the same. The Appellant was served with a show cause notice alongwith a copy of his confessional statement. The Appellant denied the allegations made against him in the show cause notice and submitted that the concerned authority had already held an inquiry in this regard and after recording the evidence had concluded that no charges are proved against the Appellant. The Appellant was served with a subsequent show cause notice asking him to submit additional reply, if any. The Appellant submitted additional reply, stating that he was forced to give self incriminating confessional statement which deserves to be discarded on account of being false and made under coercion. The officiating officer had opined in favour of dropping the proceedings against the Appellant. The services of the Appellant was terminated. Challenging the termination order, the Appellant filed an application under Section 14 of the Armed Forces Tribunal Act, 2007 before the Tribunal. Even when the matter was pending before the Tribunal, the Appellant filed petition before the High Court. The High Court disposed of the writ petition with liberty to the Appellant to file representation before the concerned authority. However, the Appellant did not prefer any representation before the concerned authority thereof. The Tribunal dismissed the Appellant's application as being devoid of any merit. The miscellaneous application filed by the Appellant seeking leave to appeal to the Supreme Court was also dismissed. Aggrieved thereof, the Appellant filed an appeal.

Held, while allowing the appeal partly:

(i) After having rightly appraised the evidence on record and the law dealing with the subject, the Tribunal dismissed the application filed by the Appellant, thereby affirming his dismissal from service. There was no perversity in the findings of the Tribunal. However, with regard to infliction of punishment of dismissal from service, the Tribunal could have kept in view the long service of the Appellant. 9

(ii) When the dismissal order was passed in case of the Appellant, the General Officer Commanding could have taken into account the unblemished service record of the Appellant and his long service. If an order of discharge would have been inflicted against the Appellant, he still would have been restricted from continuing in service and at the same time, the Appellant, who had served diligently for more than 17 years, would have been granted with the benefits accrued on his service rendered so far. [10]

(iii) The dismissal order passed against the Appellant was within the powers of the concerned authorities. However, as far as the dismissal from service is concerned, it is an extreme punishment imposed against the

Appellant. The Appellant has to thrive in civil life by doing an appropriate job suitable to his qualification. The punishment of dismissal was modified from service into discharge from service. [11]

CHAPTER EIGHTEEN

Union of India (UOI) and Ors. vs. R. Metri (04.04.2022 - SC) : MANU/SC/0407/2022

Relative Section:

Armed Forces Tribunal Act 2007 - Section 15, Armed Forces Tribunal Act 2007 - Section 15(4); Army Act, 1950 - Section 63, Army Act, 1950 - Section 69; Constitution of India - Article 20(3); Evidence Act; Indian Penal Code, 1860 (IPC) - Section 406, Indian Penal Code, 1860 (IPC) - Section 420; Prevention Of Corruption Act, 1988 - Section 7.

Hon'bleJudges/Coram:

L. Nageswara Rao and B.R. Gavai, JJ.

Equivalent Citation: 2022(233)AIC20, AIR2022SC1661, 2022 (121) ACC 368, 2022 (2) ALT (Crl.) 240 (A.P.), 2022(2)BomCR(Cri)297, 2022(2)Crimes126(SC), 2022/INSC/383, 2022(3)N.C.C.447, 2022(2) RLW 1392 (SC), (2022)6SCC525, 2022(2)SCT459(SC), 2022(3)SLR549(SC), 2022(2)UC1317

Case Reference:

Union of India (UOI) and Ors. v. Sandeep Kumar and Ors. MANU/SC/1259/2019;

The State of Bombay v. Kathi Kalu Oghad and Ors. MANU/SC/0134/1961;

Chandra Kumar Chopra v. Union of India (UOI) and Ors. MANU/SC/0424/2012;

Sahadevan and Ors. v. State of Tamil Nadu MANU/SC/0499/2012

NumberofPagesintheOriginalJudgment:14

Case Note:

Criminal - Acquittal - Legality - Section 7 of the Prevention of Corruption Act, 1988 (P.C. Act) -Present cross-appeals challenge the judgments and orders passed by the learned Armed Forces Tribunal - Whether Respondent-officer deserves to be acquitted of the offence punishable under Section 7 of the P.C. Act?

Facts:

Criminal Appeal is filed by the Union of India and others challenging that part of the judgment and order of the learned AFT, vide which the learned AFT, while setting aside the order of conviction, under Section 7 of the P.C. Act read with Section 69 of the Army Act, 1950 ("the Army Act") and the sentence of cashiering from service and suffering of rigorous imprisonment for one year, dated 28th April, 2013 passed by the General Court Martial ("GCM"), has convicted the Respondent-Major R. Metriunder Section 63 of the Army Act, and in turn, sentenced him to punishment of forfeiture of seniority of rank of Major and of severe reprimand. The learned AFT has also directed that the Respondent-officer be reinstated in service, with no pay and allowance for the period he remained out of service, but, without any service break. Another Criminal Appeal have been filed by the Respondent-officer, aggrieved by that part of the said judgment and order of the learned AFT, convicting him for offence punishable under Section 63 of the Army Act and sentencing him to punishment of forfeiture of seniority of rank and of severe reprimand.

Held, while dismissing the appeal

1. If the view taken by the learned AFT is found to be a plausible one, it will not be permissible for this Court to interfere with the same only because this Court finds the other view to be more probable/plausible. Equally, unless the finding of the learned AFT is found to be perverse or impossible, an interference would not be justified. [33]

2. The extra-judicial confession is a weak piece of evidence. Unless such a confession is found to be voluntary, trustworthy and reliable, the conviction solely on the basis of the same, without corroboration, would not be justified. [45]

3. It could thus be seen that a single officer like the Respondent-officer cannot declare a candidate medically fit, if he is otherwise not. His evidence would show that, the team like the one of which the Respondent-officer was a member, only assists the independent members in the conduct of tests, measurements and the medical examination. [47]

4. All the three witnesses have admitted that they had no knowledge if any candidate, declared fit by the Respondent-officer, was subsequently found to have been medically unfit. All the three witnesses have also admitted that there was no material to establish that the amount, which was deposited in the account of the Respondent-officer and his father-in-law was an amount received as illegal gratification. [48]

5. No error could be found with the findings of the learned AFT that the Respondent-officer deserves to be acquitted of the offence punishable under Section 7 of the P.C. Act. [49]

6. That leaves present Court with the appeals of the Respondent-officer. [50]

7. Perusal of the evidence of P.W. 10-Varalakshmi Srinivas and P.W. 12-Major D. Srinivas would reveal that they have stated in their evidence, that since the wife of the Respondent-officer had given birth to a girl child on 16th February, 2009, he wanted to rush to his native place at Dharwad and did not have sufficient funds. As such, he had requested P.W. 12-Major D. Srinivas to give a loan of Rs. 20,000, which amount was deposited by P.W. 10-Varalakshmi Srinivas in the account of the Respondent-officer, on the instructions of her husband P.W. 12-Major D. Srinivas. From the evidence of P.W. 12-Major D. Srinivas, it would reveal that on his return from his native place, the Respondent-officer had returned the said amount. [51]

8. Insofar as the amount of Rs. 65,000 is concerned, P.W. 8-Major BSRK Prasad, in his evidence, has stated that he had taken a loan of Rs. 65,000 from the father-in-law of the Respondent-officer for purchase of a plot of land. The amount of Rs. 65,000 deposited by him in the account of the father-in-law of the Respondent-officer was towards repayment of the said loan amount. [52]

9. It could thus be seen that the Respondent-officer had discharged the burden to prove, as to how the said amount of Rs. 20,000 was deposited in his account and as to how the amount of Rs. 65,000 was deposited in the account of his father-in-law. As such, that part of the order, which convicts the Respondent-officer for the offence punishable Under Section 63 of the Army Act, is not sustainable. [53]

10. Criminal Appeal filed on behalf of the Union of India and others is dismissed. Criminal Appeal filed on behalf of the Appellant-Major R. Metri are allowed. The impugned judgment and order passed by the learned AFT, convicting the Appellant-Major R. Metri for the offence punishable Under Section 63 of the Army Act and sentencing him to forfeiture of seniority of

rank and of severe reprimand is quashed and set aside. The Appellant-Major R. Metri is directed to be reinstated forthwith with continuity of service. However, in the facts and circumstances of the case, the Appellant-Major R. Metri will not be entitled for back-wages for the period during which he was out of employment. [54]

CHAPTER NINETEEN

Union of India (UOI) and Ors. vs. Sandeep Kumar and Ors. (13.09.2019 - SC) : MANU/SC/1259/2019

Relative Section:

Air Force Act; Armed Forces Tribunal Act 2007 - Section 15, Section 30,Section 133; Naval Discipline Act; Army Act, 1950 - Section 52(a); Army Rules, 1954 - Rule 58; Code of Criminal Procedure, 1973 (CrPC) - Section 164,Section 313, Section 342; Indian Evidence Act, 1872 - Section 1, Section 15, Section 25, Section 26, Section 27, Section 65; Indian Navy (Discipline) Act, 1934; Indian Penal Code, 1860 (IPC) - Section 34

Hon'bleJudges/Coram:

L. Nageswara Rao and Hemant Gupta, JJ.

Equivalent Citation: 2020(208)AIC183, 2019(4)Crimes121(SC), 2019/INSC/1030, 2019(4)MLJ(Crl)70, 2020(1)N.C.C.236, 2019(12)SCALE486, (2019)10SCC496, (2020)1SCC(LS)126, [2019]12SCR415, 2019(4)SCT422(SC), 2020(2)SLR257(SC)

Case Reference:

Ajay Kumar Singh and Ors. v. The Flag Officer Commanding-in-Chief and Ors. MANU/SC/0765/2016; Keya Mukherjee v. Magma Leasing Limited and Anr. MANU/SC/7473/2008; Jai Dev v. The State of Punjab MANU/SC/0134/1962; Nar Singh v. State of Haryana MANU/SC/1004/2014; Wasim Khan v. The State of Uttar Pradesh MANU/SC/0022/1956; Bhoor Singh and Anr. v. State of Punjab MANU/SC/0109/1974; Santosh Kumar Singh v. State thr. CBI MANU/SC/0801/2010

NumberofPagesintheOriginalJudgment:16

Case Note:

Defence - Conviction - Theft of pistols - Armed Forces Tribunal set aside order of conviction and sentence and of dismissal consequent to District Court Martial (DCM) proceedings conducted against Respondents on charge of theft of pistols - Tribunal passed order for reinstatement of both Accused - Hence, present appeal - Whether Tribunal exceeded its jurisdiction while setting aside order of conviction passed by DCM.

Facts:

The Armed Forces Tribunal setting aside the order of conviction and sentence and of dismissal consequent to District Court Martial proceedings conducted against the Respondents on charge of theft of pistol. The Tribunal passed an order for reinstatement of both the Accused but it was also ordered that the Accused shall not be entitled to any back wages for the period they were out of service. The other two appeals are against the order passed by the Tribunal declining back wages to the Accused in those appeals.

Held, while allowing the appeal:

(i) The prosecution case was based upon written confessional statements made by Accused. In addition to the confessional statements, oral confessions were made before Squadron Commander and Commandant. Commandant had not been cross-examined in respect of any involuntary nature of the confession or that he was the person who has given beatings to the Accused as averred by them in their statements under Rule 58 of Army Rules. The Accused without asking any question to any of the prosecution witness that they had given beatings as alleged by them in their statements, could not doubt the consistent evidence of the prosecution witnesses. Therefore, the retraction of the confessional statements made in their statement under Rule 58 of Rules was of no consequence when the prosecution witnesses had not been cross-examined in respect of involuntary nature of the confessions. The statement of witnesses of different ranks, could not be doubted by the Tribunal. The findings of the Tribunal were in fact based on ipse dixit of the Tribunal. [36]

(ii) The Accused had tried to create doubt on the prosecution story on the basis of the fact that the originals of handwritten slip had not been produced. Prosecution witness had deposed that original of such slip had been lost during transit whereas the scanned copy was the true copy of the original which the witness had seen. Such statement was supported by statements of prosecution witness who had found the slip and prosecution witness who had recovered the cardboard shoebox. Still further, before the DCM, the Accused had not disputed the production of the slips by way of secondary evidence. Therefore, no reason not to take into consideration such slips in evidence as prosecution witnesses were the persons who had seen the originals and had also deposed that the scanned copies are the same as of originals. Therefore, the Tribunal erred in law in reversing the findings recorded by the DCM while exercising appellate jurisdiction under Section 15 of the Act. [41]

(iii) Section 15 of the Armed Forces Tribunal Act, 2007 confers wide power on the Tribunal so as to allow an appeal against conviction by a Court Martial where the finding of the Court Martial was legally not sustainable due to any reason; the finding involves wrong decision on a question of law or there was a material irregularity in the course of the trial resulting in miscarriage of justice. Even though the power of the Tribunal is wide but it was not merely a different opinion on the appreciation of the evidence to interfere with the findings recorded by the Court Martial. The first ground of interference was whether the finding of the Court Martial was legally not sustainable. Therefore, to exercise such power, there had to be error of law by the Court Martial which would confer jurisdiction on the Tribunal to interfere against the conviction recorded by the Court Martial. The second ground was wrong application on a question of law. However, the Tribunal, in the present case, had committed grave error in interfering with the finding of the Court Martial by misreading an Army Order. There was no material irregularity pointed out by the Tribunal inasmuch as the irregularity pointed out is with regard to confessional statements by Military Officer which is not a bar either under the Evidence Act or under the Army Order issued under the Act. The Tribunal could re-appreciate evidence to find out if any findings of the Court Martial was legally not sustainable due to any reason; or that the finding involves wrong decision on a question of law or there was a material irregularity in the course of the trial resulting in miscarriage of justice. But such wide powers did not confer jurisdiction to the Tribunal to reverse the findings merely because it finds that different view was possible. [46]

(iv) The Tribunal exceeded its jurisdiction while setting aside the order of conviction passed by the DCM. [47]

CHAPTER TWENTY

Union of India (UOI) and Ors. vs. R. Karthik (21.01.2020 - SC) : MANU/SC/0060/2020

Relative Section:

Air Force Act, 1950; Armed Forces Tribunal Act 2007 - Section 3(f), Section 15, Section 15(6), Section 30; Army Act, 1950; Navy Act, 1957 - Section 45(a), Navy Act, 1957 - Section 74.

Hon'bleJudges/Coram:

L. Nageswara Rao and Hemant Gupta

Equivalent Citation: [2020(166)FLR393], 2020/INSC/62, 2020(2)JCC977, (2020)2SCC782, (2020) 1SCC(LS)335, [2020]1SCR105, 2020(1)SCT728(SC), 2020(4)SLR253(SC), 2020(1)UC471

Case Reference:

NumberofPagesintheOriginalJudgment:6

Case Note:

Defence - Punishment - Substitution of - Section 45(a) of Navy Act, 1957 - Sailor entered in Naval service and assigned duties in Pay Office for preparation of pay bills and payment of salaries and maintenance of records - Complaint was made requesting strict possible action against Sailor - Commanding Officer found charges to be proved of offence under Section 45(a) of Act and recommended detention and deprivation of First Good Conduct Badge - However, Chief of Naval Staff passed order of dismissal of Sailor from Naval Service and deprivation of First Good Conduct Badge - Original application was filed before Tribunal against said order - Tribunal set aside order of dismissal but substituting it with punishment of detention and maintaining second part of sentence i.e. deprivation of First Good

Conduct Badge - Hence, present appeal - Whether substituted punishment awarded by Tribunal warrant any interference.

Facts:

The Sailor entered in Naval service and assigned duties in the Pay Office for preparation of pay bills and payment of salaries and maintenance of records. An unfortunate incident happened when superior officer made a complaint requesting strict possible action against the Sailor. The Commanding Officer found the charges to be proved of an offence under Section 45(a) of the Navy Act, 1957 and recommended the detention for a period of 60 days and deprivation of First Good Conduct Badge. However, the Chief of Naval Staff passed an order of dismissal of Sailor from Naval Service and deprivation of First Good Conduct Badge. It was the said order which was challenged by the Sailor by way of an Original Application before the Tribunal. The Tribunal held that the sentence of dismissal from service awarded to the applicant by the Chief of Naval Staff was disproportionate and excessive. The Tribunal partly modified the punishment by setting aside the order of dismissal but substituting it with punishment of detention and maintaining second part of sentence i.e. deprivation of First Good Conduct Badge.

Held, while dismissing the appeal:

(i) None of the witnesses had deposed regarding hitting of superior officer by the Sailor. The superior officer was not examined either before the Investigation Officer or the Executive Officer nor he had been made available for cross-examination as per the proceedings produced before us. It had also come on record that the superior officer had been found to be guilty for using abusive language against the Sailor. [9]

(ii) Even though, the superior officer had used abusive language but the Sailor was not expected to retort and hit the superior officer. The conduct of the Sailor could not be condoned in any manner. [12]

(iii) In terms of provisions of the AFT Act, the Tribunal was competent to substitute the findings in the disciplinary proceedings leading to dismissal of the Sailor and to substitute and/or mitigate the punishment awarded. Therefore, the order passed by the Tribunal to set aside the dismissal was within the jurisdiction of the Tribunal finding that the punishment imposed was disproportionate to the misconduct. This Court in appellate jurisdiction under Section 30 of the AFT Act would be slow in interfering with the substituted punishment, unless the order passed by the Tribunal was found to be arbitrary, unreasonable or capricious. The view taken by the Tribunal was not patently illegal warranting interference in the present appeal. [13]

Disposition:

Appeal Dismissed

CHAPTER TWENTY-ONE

21.Yogesh Pathania vs. Union of India (UOI) and Ors. (08.01.2019 - SC) : MANU/SC/0026/2019

Relative Section:

Armed Forces Tribunal Act 2007 - Section 15, Section 19, Section 30, Section 30(1), Section 31, Section 31(1); Air Force Act, 1950 - Section 40, Section 65, Section 161(2)

Hon'bleJudges/Coram:

Dr. D.Y. Chandrachud and Hemant Gupta.

Equivalent Citation: 2019(1)ESC117(SC), 2019(1)ESC35(SC), 2019/INSC/33, 2019(1)SCALE254, (2019)4SCC311, (2019)1SCC(LS)647, 2019 (9) SCJ 682, [2019]1SCR161, 2019(1)SCT512(SC), 2019(1)SLJ97(SC), 2019(1)UC55

Case Reference:

NumberofPagesintheOriginalJudgment: 5

Case Note:

Service - Punishment - Sections 30 and 31 of Armed Forces Tribunal Act, 2007 - Present appeal seeking leave to appeal arose out of an order passed by Armed Forces Tribunal confirming findings of District Court Martial (DCM) that, Appellant be given punishment of rigorous imprisonment for five months and ordered dismissal from service - Whether imposition of punishment against Appellant was in accordance with law.

Facts:

Allegations against Appellant were that he misbehaved with senior officers. Appeal before Tribunal was directed against findings and sentence awarded by District Court Martial ('DCM') and also against rejection of his statutory complaint under Section 161(2) of Air Force Act, 1950 by Chief of Air Staff. DCM was initiated on account of an incident on intervening night and 23rd May, 2009 wherein a breach of good order of Air Force discipline was created by Module II airmen trainees attached to NTTI and Accounts Conversion Course trainees in TV Room, over change of TV channel. A Court of Inquiry was conducted followed by summary of evidences. Thereafter Appellant was tried by DCM on seven charges of misconduct. DCM had found Appellant guilty. Before DCM, prosecution examined 14 witnesses, whereas Appellant examined 3 witnesses in defence. After examining evidence on record, Appellant was given punishment of rigorous imprisonment for five months and also an order of dismissal from service was passed. Such punishment was subject to modification of punishment of rigorous imprisonment being reduced to a period of two months. It was thereafter a statutory complaint was filed which was also dismissed. Tribunal, in appeal under Section 15 of Act, examined evidence led by parties and found no error in findings recorded by DCM and consequently dismissed appeal. It was, thereafter, present appeal with an application for permission to file appeal had been preferred.

Held, while dismissing the appeal

1. Question as to whether Warrant Officer (PW11) had given slaps to Appellant was a question of fact. Learned Tribunal had examined statements of witnesses to upheld charges as proved. Thus, stand of Appellant that he was slapped was not made out from evidence on record. Tribunal had re-appreciated evidence and concurred with findings of DCM. [11]

2. Even though, Tribunal had recorded a finding of fact in respect of misconduct alleged against Appellant. View taken by Tribunal was a plausible view and therefore did not warrant any interference in appeal in terms of jurisdiction vested in this Court under Sections 30 and 31 of Act. [12]

3. In terms of Section 31 of Act, an appeal to this Court was maintainable with leave of Tribunal and such leave could be granted on ground "that a point of law of general public importance" or "it appears to Supreme Court that point was one which ought to be considered by that Court". Point on which this Court would exercise jurisdiction was a point of law of general

public importance. There was no point of law of general public importance involved which might warrant grant of leave to Appellant. Appeal dismissed. [13]

Disposition:

Appeal Dismised

Adv. Jayprakash Somani's Videos On Law

Adv. Jayprakash Somani's Videos on Law on Youtube- 'jaysomani64' channel.

1) SLP in Supreme Court / Special Leave Petitions in the Supreme Court of India

2) Transfer of Civil & Criminal Cases by the Supreme Court of India / Transfer of Matrimonial Cases

3) Appellate Jurisdiction of the Supreme Court of India

4) Jurisdictions of the Supreme Court of India

5) Public Interest Litigation in the Supreme Court of India / PIL in Supreme Court

6) Article 32 Writ Petitions in the Supreme Court of India

7) Bail Matters Top 10 Supreme Court Cases

8) FIR Quashing in High Court & Supreme Court

9) Bail & Anticipatory Bail Matters in Supreme Court

10) Insolvency & Bankruptcy Matters in the Supreme Court

11) Insolvency & Bankruptcy Code 2016 Part 1

12) Insolvency & Bankruptcy Code 2016 Part 2

13) Insolvency & Bankruptcy Code 2016 Part 3

14) Corporate Liquidation Process

15) Supreme Court Rules & Procedures Webinar of 2.5 hour on Zoom

16) RDDBFI Act, 1993 (Introduction)

17) The Indian Contact Act 1872

18) Negotiable Instruments Act (Introduction)

19) How to avoid matrimonial disputes& some more videos

20) SEBI Matters in the Supreme Court

21) Matrimonial Matters: Supreme Court's 20 Case Laws

22) Consumer Matters Supreme Court's 20 Case Laws

23) Service Matters Supreme Court's 20 Case Laws

24) How to Search Lawyer for Your Matter

25) Property Matters Supreme Court's 20 Case Laws

26) Bail Matters: Supreme Court's 20 Case Laws

27) Supreme Court / High Court Vacation Benches

28) 69000 Teacher's Recruitment Matters of UP Government in the Supreme Court

29) Contempt of Court Matters in the Supreme Court

30) Advocate Act's Matters in the Supreme Court

31) Business Law Matters in the Supreme Court

32) Banking Matters in the Supreme Court

33) Labour Law Matters in the Supreme Court

34) Arbitration Matters in the Supreme Court

35) Careers in Law -Zoom Webinar by Adv. Jayprakash Somani

36) Civil Matters in the Supreme Court

37) Consumer Protection Act | Consumer Matters in the Supreme Court

38) Corporate Matters in the Supreme Court

39) Criminal Matters in the Supreme Court

40) Role of Respondent in the Supreme Court of India

41) Motor Vehicle Accident Matters in Supreme Court with case laws

42) Article 131 Original Suits in Supreme Court

43) PIL in Supreme Court/ Public Interest Litigations in the Supreme Court of India'

44) CAB Citizenship Amendment Bill is not Unconstitutional

45) Supreme Court of India Cases & Process – Marathi

46) Legal Services Export / Export of Legal Services

47) Transfer of Matrimonial Cases by the Supreme Court of India

48) Public Interest Litigation PIL

49) The Specific Relief Act (Introduction)

50) Corporate Insolvency Resolution Process CIRP

51) ABMM's Career 5 - Careers in Law

52) Transfer of cases by Supreme Court

53) Writ Petitions in High Court & Supreme Court of India

54) Supreme Court Jurisdictions - Appeals, SLP, Writ Petitions, Transfer, Original, Review, Curative

55) LEGAL INDIA TV Show: Cases Handled in Supreme Court

56) Corporate Liquidation Process

57) Legal Services Export / Export of Legal Services

58) Corporate Laws

59) Election Matters- Supreme Court's 20 Case Laws

60) Companies Act, 2013

62) Competition Act, 2002

63) Banking Matters - Supreme Court's 20 Case Laws

64) Election Matters in the Supreme Court

65) Armed Forces Tribunal Matters in the Supreme Court

66) Compassionate Appointment Service matter

67) Foreign Exchange Management Act FEMA

68) Foreign Trade Policy 2021-26 Proposed

69) Customs Act 1962

70) Narcotic Drugs and Psychotropic Substances Act, 1985 NDPS Act

71) Foreign Trade Development & Regulation Act, 1992

72) How to Search Good Advocate in the Supreme Court of India

73) Sr. Adv Vikas Singh's Interview in Nani Palkhivala Wednesday Law Club

74) Indian Penal Code (I. P. C.)

75) Criminal Procedure Code (Cr. P. C.)

76) Commercial Courts & International Arbitration - by Mr. Jaideep Gupta, Senior Advocate in Nani Palkhivala Wednesday Law Club

77) Sr. Adv Ranji Thomos in Nani Palkhivala Wednesday Law Club

78) Urgent Matters in Supreme Court during vacations

79) 498A Bail Matters in Supreme Court

81) 376 Bail Matters in Supreme Court

82) 302, 304, 307, 308 Bail Matters in Supreme Court

83) 138, 420 Bail Matters in Supreme Court

84) POCSO Act Bail Matters in Supreme Court

85) NDPS Act Bail Matters in Supreme Court

86) What is ED (Enforcement Directorate)?

87) Prevention of Money Laundering Act, 2002 (PMLA Act)

88) Insolvency & Bankruptcy Code- Supreme Court Case Laws. Webinar in Nani Palkhivala Wednesday Law Club

89) What is NCLT & NCLAT?

90) Acquittal from 376- Supreme Court's some case laws in Nani Palkhivala Wednesday Law Club dt 28.7.22

91) Insolvency & Bankruptcy in India

92) Can we file case directly in the Supreme Court?

93) Adv. Anuja Pethia has cleared AOR Exam 2021 with 77% marks - Her interview in Nani Palkhivala Wednesday Law Club

94) Customs Act - Supreme Court Case Laws & Interview of AOR Adv. Anuja Pethia in Nani Palkhivala Law Club.

95) The Uttar Pradesh Public Service Tribunals Act, 1976

96) POCSO Act - Supreme Court Case Laws & Interview of AOR Adv. Shoumendu Mukharji & Adv. Nishant Verma in Nani Palkhivala Law Club.

97) Who Can Trigger CIRP Process Under Insolvency Law of India

98) The Uttar Pradesh Government Servant Discipline and Appeal Rules, 1999

99) CIRP Application Under Sec 7 by FC

100) Information Technology Act 2000

101) Uttar Pradesh Recruitment of Dependants of Government Servants Dying in Harness Rules, 1974

102) Foreign Exchange Management Act 1999 & Supreme Court's Case Laws on FEMA & Leading Case of AOR Exam in Nani Palkhivala Law Club.

103) Arbitration and Conciliation Act 1996 & It's Supreme Court Case Laws in Nani Palkhivala Wednesday Law Club.

104) Narcotic Drugs & Psychotropic Substances Act 1985 (NDPS Act) & It's Supreme Court Case Laws in Nani Palkhivala Wednesday Law Club.

105) Recovery of Debts and Bankruptcy Act 1993

106) Uttar Pradesh Land Revenue Code 2006

107) CIRP Application Under Sec 9 by OC

108) CIRP Application Under Sec 10 by CD

109) Hindu Succession Act, 1956

110) Maharashtra Civil Services Rules, 1981

111) Indian Contract Act, 1872 & Supreme Court's Case Laws" in Nani Palkhiwala Wednesday Law Club

112) Securities and Exchange Board of India Act, 1992 i. e. SEBI Act 1992 & Case Laws on Insiders Trading" in Nani Palkhiwala Wednesday Law Club

113) Moratorium Under Section 14 of IBC, 2016

114) Hindu Marriage Act, 1955

115) Maharashtra Land Revenue Code, 1966

116) 64 Leading Cases of AOR Exam Session 1 :- Cases 1 to16 in Nani Palkhiwala Wednesday Law Club

117) 64 Leading Cases of AOR Exam Session 2: Cases 17 to 32 in Nani Palkhivala Wednesday Law Club

118) 64 Leading Cases of AOR Examination Session 3: Cases 33 to 48 in Nani Palkhivala Wednesday Law Club

119) 64 Leading Cases of AOR Exam Session 4: Cases 49 to 64 in Nani Palkhivala Wednesday Law Club

120) Labour Laws of India: Part 1 - 4 New Labour Law Codes of India

121) New Labour Laws Part 2 The Code on Wages, 2019

122) New Labour Laws Part 3:- The Code on Social Security, 2020

123) Argue in English Fluently & Confidently - Two months online course.

124) SLP Admission in the Supreme Court. 2023 (Hindi)

125) Transfer of Petitions from the Supreme Court (Hindi)

126) Review Petition in the Supreme Court.(Hindi)

127) Recovery of debts from the Company (Hindi)

128) How to search 'Good Insolvency & Bankruptcy Consultant?' (HINDI)

129) Curative Petition in the Supreme Court

130) AFT Appeals in the Supreme Court (HINDI)

131) NCLAT's Appeals in the Supreme Court.

132) Transfer Petition: Which matters can we transfer?

133) SLP Types of SLP in the Supreme court of India (English).

134) Argue in English Fluently and Confidently in the High Court & Supreme Court'.

List Of Adv. Jayprakash Somani's Published Books

1. Supreme Court of India's Leading Case Laws on 'Insolvency & Bankruptcy Code 2016'

2. Bail Matters – Supreme Court's Latest Leading Case Laws

3. Arbitration Matters- Supreme Court's Latest Leading Case Laws

4. Property Matters - Supreme Court's Latest Leading Case Laws

5. Matrimonial Matters- Supreme Court's Latest Leading Case Laws

6. Election Matters- Supreme Court's Latest Leading Case Laws

7.SEBI Matters- Supreme Court's Latest Leading Case Laws

8. Banking Matters- Supreme Court's Latest Leading Case Laws

9. Service Matters- Supreme Court's Latest Leading Case Laws

10. Contempt of Court Matters- Supreme Court's Latest Leading Case Laws

11. Consumer Protection Matters- Supreme Court's Latest Leading Case Laws

12. Corporate Law- Supreme Court's Latest Leading Case Laws

13. Supreme Court's AOR Exam- Leading Cases

14. Armed Force Tribunal - Supreme Court's Latest Leading Case Laws

15. Acquittal From 376 - Supreme Court's Latest Leading Case Laws

16. Negotiable instrument – Supreme Court's Latest Leading Case Laws

17. Contract Act- Supreme Court's Latest Leading Case Laws

18. Insider trading- Supreme Court's Latest Leading Case Laws

19. Foreign Exchange and Management Act- Supreme Court's Latest Leading Case Laws

20. Income Tax Act- Supreme Court's Latest Leading Case Laws

21. Company Law- Supreme Court's Latest Leading Case Laws

22. Competition & Monopoly Matters- Supreme Court's Latest Leading Case Laws

23. Compassionate Appointment- Service Matters- Supreme Court's Latest Leading Case Laws

24. Compulsory Retirement- Service Matters- Supreme Court's Latest Leading Case Laws

25. Voluntary Retirement- Service Matters- Supreme Court's Latest Leading Case Laws

26. Removal/Dismissal/Termination from Service- Supreme Court's Latest Leading Case Laws

27. Seniority- Service Matter- Supreme Court's Latest Leading Case Laws

28. Promotion- Service Matter- Supreme Court's Latest Leading Case Laws

29. Equal Pay for Equal Work- Service Matter- Supreme Court's Latest Leading Case Laws

30. Condition of Service- Service Matter- Supreme Court's Latest Leading Case Laws

31. Customs Act- Supreme Court's Leading Case Laws

32. Information Technology Act- Supreme Court's Leading Case Laws

33. SEC. 125 CR. P. C.- Supreme Court's Leading Case Laws

34. SEC. 498A OF I. P. C.- Supreme Court's Leading Case Laws

35. MOTOR VEHICLE ACT- Supreme Court's Leading Case Laws

36. CONDITION OF SERVICE- SERVICE MATTER- Supreme Court's Leading Case Laws

37. SUSPENSION- SERVICE MATTER- Supreme Court's Leading Case Laws

38. Reservation in SC, ST, OBC- Service Matter- Supreme Court's Leading Case Laws

39. NARCOTIC DRUGS AND PSYCHOTROPIC SUBSTANCES (NDPS) ACT - Supreme Court of India's Latest Leading Case Laws

40. SEC 302 IPC - Supreme Court of India's Latest Leading Case Laws

41. PROTECTION OF CHILDREN FROM SEXUAL OFFENCES ACT (POCSO) - Supreme Court of India's Latest Leading Case Laws

42. PMLA ACT BAIL MATTERS - Supreme Court of India's Leading Case Laws

43. SEC 376 BAIL MATTERS - Supreme Court of India's Leading Case Laws

44. SEC 302 BAIL MATTERS - Supreme Court of India's Leading Case Laws

45. POCSO ACT BAIL MATTERS - Supreme Court of India's Leading Case Laws

46. JUVENILE JUSTICE ACT- Supreme Court of India's Leading Case Laws

47. TRANSFER OF PROPERTY ACT- Supreme Court of India's Leading Case Laws

48. PROFESSIONAL ETHICS OF ADVOCATES- AOR EXAM- SUPREME COURT'S LEADING CASE LAWS

49. WHITE COLLAR CRIME- SUPREME COURT'S LEADING CASE LAWS

50. SEC 302 BAIL MATTERS- SUPREME COURT'S LEADING CASE LAWS

51. SEC 7 IBC 2016 - SUPREME COURT'S LATEST LEADING CASE LAW

52. ADVERSE POSSESSION IN PROPERTY MATTER - SUPREME COURT'S LATEST LEADING CASE LAWS

Books are available online in India

1. Notion Press: https://notionpress.com/author/jayprakash_somani

2. Amazon: https://www.amazon.in/s?k=jayprakash+somani

3. Flipkart: https://www.flipkart.com/search?q=Jayprakash%20Somani

Books are available online at International Market

4. Amazon International: https://www.amazon.com/s?k=jayprakash+somani

5. Amazon United Kingdom: https://www.amazon.co.uk/s?k=jayprakash+somani

6. E-Books/Kindle edition at National & International Level: https://www.amazon.in/s?k=jaypraksh+somani

www.ingramcontent.com/pod-product-compliance
Lightning Source LLC
LaVergne TN
LVHW021159160826
845679LV00024B/2173

* 9 7 9 8 8 9 1 8 6 7 1 2 3 *